STILL
whispers

meditations to help you calm
the atmosphere of your life
and find abundance

PHIL FARRAND

This book was printed in the United States of America. For information on obtaining additional copies of this book or other writings by Phil Farrand please visit:

http://philfarrand.com

Dedicated to all those with whom I have been privileged to share a meal and community.

10 9 8 7 6 5 4

Table of Contents

an *exercise* in FUTILITY

In many ways, this book is an exercise in futility.

Of the billions of humans who live on this planet, the great majority will never know it exists.

Among those who do, most will never come into direct contact with it and even if they do, they will never venture past the cover.

Some will look inside, scan the table of contents and then put it down.

Others will flip through a few pages and only read a sentence here or there before quickly concluding they don't need what it offers.

Of those who remain, some will actually read a chapter or two but then distraction will hustle them away.

Many of those who venture farther will choose some moment to toss it aside with indifference or disgust or anger.

For some, the mere fact that I quote the Bible will be enough to raise a dismissive snarl within them.

Even sadder will be those who make it to the final chapter and afterwards use the knowledge solely to identify the faults of others. In those situations, this book will do more harm than good.

Most tortuous, though, are those seekers who will understand perfectly what I illustrate in the coming chapters. Yet, they will never consistently apply it in their lives. They will know there is more but they will never experience it. (For this, I apologize. I have increased your suffering and I knew it would be so.)

In the presence of such vanity, it would be easy to abandon this effort and continue the approach that I have used for many years, starting with my daughter.

Set aside a time once a week.

Meet at a restaurant.

Enjoy a meal.

Share our lives.

Listen, guide, grow, teach, learn, give and receive.

Experience community.

This is the *only* approach that I have seen that can help another see all that this life has to offer.

Instruction *en masse* rarely works (for reasons that should become clear in future chapters). "Broadcasting" these concepts like a farmer broadcasts seed simply means that most of the seed will die or will be swept away or stolen long before it can take root.

Why, then, did I spend almost year of my spare time to write this book if I am so convinced of the ineffectiveness and futility of this approach?

Because a whisper within that tells me it's time.

Because there are those on the same path as I, some farther, some nearer, some behind, some ahead, some parallel, some tangential and there may be something here that may assist.

To you, I say, welcome.

I have no idea the route that brought this book to you. Now that it has; now that you have begun...

Don't stop.

I have done my best to be clear, accessible, brief and easy to remember — to write this as if we were enjoying a series of meals together. I have not tried to cover every topic exhaustively. Nor have I tried to counter every argument. If you are the type of who needs to interrupt most statements with "yeah...but," this may not be worthwhile for you.

And, while I hesitate to discourage you from this endeavor so near the beginning, you should expect this to be difficult. There will be resistance. There will be distractions.

Remember the words of Jesus:

"Enter through the narrow gate. For wide is the gate and broad is the road that leads to destruction, and many enter through it. But small is the gate and narrow the road that leads to life, and only a few find it." (Matthew 7:13-14 NIV)

CLUB ubiquity

Almost everyone knows that Jesus told us to love our enemies.

While we could spend a great deal of time discussing how this benefits us, I would rather focus on the important truth that this command reveals about creation.

In the Matthew 5:43-48, Jesus says that we should love our enemies as a way of following God's pattern. Jesus observes that God has provided sun and rain to every inhabitant on Earth and we should follow this pattern and treat everyone with equal attention and compassion.

Sun and rain are crucial resources to life in an agrarian society. Those who heard Jesus speak that day understood that he was abolishing the notion that God has parceled humanity into two clubs, blessing one with natural resources while depriving the other. Instead, God has built a world rich in beauty and wealth and made those resources available to all.

There is only one "club." The Divine has woven resources into this world and made them available to all. They are ubiquitous. Every human has always and will always have a membership in this club.

The principles that I discuss in the following chapters are part of the resources that God has built into this world. It doesn't matter whether you follow the Judeo-Christian belief system or not. Even if you only take pieces of these discussions and apply them correctly, they will benefit you.

Ignore what you will. Use what you want.

Conversely, if you aren't applying these principles to your life, it won't matter if you have accepted Jesus Christ as your personal savior.

You can't gain the benefit of the resources without accessing the resources.

This is why I encourage you to keep reading even if you don't believe that God exists. You may find something here that will profit you.

Personally, I have found a great deal of wisdom in other belief systems even while I am and remain a Christian.

I hope you can do the same.

(By the way, if you aren't a Christian, the next six "framework" chapters will be tedious but please read them anyway so that we can have a basis for communication.)

abundance

Jesus said that he came so that we might have life, "and have it abundantly."

On cue, a voice from the gallery calls out, "How do you define an 'abundant' life?"

I define abundance like this:

Waking up every morning, grateful for the day;

Ready to grow;

Eager to embrace my epic;

Filled with joy;

Freed from destruction;

Surrounded by an environment of success and providing an environment of success for those around me.

I doubt there are many who would argue with this definition of abundance. Instinctively, I think we know what the abundant life should be like.

Unfortunately, we humans seem to be very good at understanding the concept while neglecting the mechanism.

This "abundant life" is a perfect example. Perhaps you've heard the verse I referenced at the start of this chapter. In John 10:10b, Jesus says, "I came that they may have life and have it abundantly." (NASB)

What we miss is the context of this verse and — in missing the context — we ultimately miss the mechanism that brings about this abundance.

The verse comes from the parable of the good shepherd (John 10:1-18). This parable continues a word picture that occurs multiple times in the Bible: God is the shepherd, we are the sheep.

In the parable, Jesus identifies himself as the good shepherd who gives his life to protect his sheep and he draws a contrast in verse ten by stating, "The thief comes only to steal and kill and destroy; I came that they may have life and have it abundantly." (John 10:10 NASB)

In other words, Jesus is really saying, "The thief comes only to steal and kill and destroy; I — as the good shepherd — have come that they (my flock) might have an abundant life."

Clearly, the promise of the abundant life is to those who are members of Jesus' flock.

And how does Jesus identify the members of his flock? What is the mechanism to indicate that certain sheep can be led by Jesus into the abundant life that he has promised?

More than once, Jesus stresses in this parable that his sheep hear and know his voice, he calls them by name and they follow him.

In Jesus' day, when he said this, there would be no question in anyone's mind that he was speaking of a daily process because…every day:

The sheep heard and knew the shepherd's voice.

He called them by name.

And he led them out.

Every day.

In other words, if you wish to find abundance in this life, learn to identify the voice of the Eternal within you and then respond to it.

Every day.

Still Whispers

Frankly, I don't remember the event but my mom has told the story enough times that I can repeat it.

My parents were missionaries. During my childhood, they served in a Bible college near the city of Manila in the Republic of the Philippines. We lived in a house on the college campus and behind our house there was a considerable stand of tall grass.

As a boy, I recall having a toy figurine with a small parachute attached. I would throw the toy into the air; the parachute would inflate and the toy would float to the ground. I would retrieve it and start the game again.

Apparently on one occasion, I tossed the toy into the air and it landed in the tall grass. According to my mom, I searched for it until I worked myself into a fit and then ran inside to tell her my plight.

She recalls being in the kitchen with one of the frequent guests who graced our home. I burst on the scene, crying, bemoaning the fact I had lost my toy.

My mother, in typical fashion, asked me if I had asked Jesus to help me find it.

When I answered no, she told me to go back outside, ask Jesus to help me find it and then start looking.

As I left the kitchen, my mother recalls that our guest was unsatisfied with this approach. In fact, he openly voiced his concern that she had set me up for failure.

"What if Philip doesn't find it?" the man asked. "What will that do to his faith?"

"He'll find it," my mom responded.

I should mention that this particular man was very much a man of faith and had traveled around the world with no money, flying into airports with no idea where he would stay or how he would even leave the airport. In every instance, God directed him and met his needs.

Because of this, I don't think our guest had any doubts that God *could* help me find the toy. I think perhaps he doubted my ability to hear God's direction because of my young age.

In any case, they continued their discussion for the next few minutes...long enough for me to trot through the kitchen with the toy in hand and a smile on my face.

While I don't remember this particular incident, I do remember my mother's repeated advice over the years to "ask

Jesus." And I *do* recall a practice of doing so that remains to this day. And I *do* remember Jesus responding.

Big things. Small things. Some serious. Some comedic. I have been blessed all my life with the habit of expecting the Divine to communicate with me.

Every day.

I could tell you lots of stories about this. It is extremely rare that a day passes when there isn't at least one whisper in my mind that begins, "Now, would probably be a good time to..." or "Weren't you planning to..."

But, I'm trying to keep this brief so I'll limit myself to just two stories—one from work, one from play.

I work as a computer consultant and I have a genre of occasional activities that I jokingly call "adding to the legend." It's when I do something that flabbergasts my co-workers. They laugh. I laugh. They shake their heads as I walk off.

I'll spare you the details but at one point several months ago, a couple of programmers whom I work with asked my advice on a problem they were having with a software package. I suggested that they secure the package with a password. At the time, I suggested they pick something simple and easy to remember. The lead programmer said the first thing that popped into his head and I told him that it sounded good to me.

About six weeks later, I wandered by the lead programmer's office. He and his fellow programmer were leaning over his computer looking frustrated. I popped in and asked if I could help.

Chagrinned, they said that they had forgotten the password and apparently hadn't written it down. It wasn't a crisis. The package would have been easy to rebuild.

I offered a few possibilities but none of them worked.

Finally I said, "Okay, just a second."

I closed my eyes, put my fists to my head, and turned off as much mental activity as I could.

Two seconds later, the password popped into my head.

"Try this," I said, smiling.

They did. It worked. They laughed. I joked, "This is why you should never tell me a password!"

I went back to my desk.

I know what you're thinking. I know you're thinking that I just have a good memory.

That might be true, except I really wasn't trying to remember the password. I knew that if I just got quiet enough with the right expectation, the Eternal would whisper it to me. And he did.

My most favorite of these whispers, though, came many years ago when my daughter was dating. To preface this story, you should know that we live several miles north of Springfield, MO, in a somewhat sparsely populated area.

She and her boyfriend were planning to go to her biological mother's house for supper but my daughter's car wouldn't start. I grabbed the jumper cables and we got the car started and—knowing that she wanted to go—I suggested that they attempt the trip. If they didn't make I would just come and pick them up.

About five minutes later, I got the call from my daughter. Her car had died. (It was the alternator, not the battery.)

I told her I was on my way.

I grabbed my keys and just as my hand hit the front door knob, I heard a little voice say...

"See, now, if you were a prophet, you would call your daughter back and tell her to wait five minutes until a blue car comes by. Then she should wave the car down and the driver will give her and her boyfriend a ride home."

At this point, I snickered because there is more than one voice in my mind and I hastily determined that the advice was not from the Divine. (I deemed it "self-centered.")

Five minutes later, as I pulled up to my daughter's car, a steel-blue automobile approached from the opposite direction. The driver slowed, rolled down the window and asked my daughter if she needed any help. The young man happened to be living with our next-door neighbors.

This is when I started laughing because the Eternal was snickering within me. He had whispered something he knew I would interpret a certain way so that he could chortle later when I realized it really was him in the first place!

I have lived long enough with the whispers that I understand God has a wonderful sense of humor.

but NOT YET *already*

Right now, "all is ready" for your life to be filled with abundance.

Truth has purchased your freedom.

Joy hovers at the edge of your awareness.

Your epic unfolds.

The Eternal still whispers, seeking communion.

The "not yet" of your life—if there is a "not yet" in your life—has nothing to do with the universe. You exist in a place of vast wonder and almost limitless potential. It is not the external that keeps you from everything this life has to offer. The "not yet" of your existence lies much closer.

The "not yet" in your life occurs solely within you.

how LIFE works

For decades, I have pondered how life works. It is part of my epic to understand how to live to the fullest of my potential.

Two experiences—two "pivot points"—have set me on my current course. (I suspect that there will be a third but that's a subject for a later chapter.)

The first pivot point came sometime around age ten when I was living in the Republic of the Philippines with my parents.

I remember strolling up the sidewalk in front of our house. The gardenia bushes that lined the walk were in bloom. As I looked in the direction of the bushes, a thought popped into my head.

"I wonder how someone would live if they acted like they believed the Bible was true."

I know now that it was the Divine whispering to me. At the time, however, I just thought it was an interesting idea and I decided to give it a try.

I should explain that I was living on a Bible college campus. I was surrounded by individuals who professed to believe the Bible was true. But even at that age, I saw many small behaviors and emotions that didn't seem very "biblical."

After all, if God is the maker of the universe and he is our "loving heavenly Father," why would anyone fear? Why worry? Why get angry?

I wasn't ready to believe that it was possible to have a belief so strong that there were never doubts. But it did seem possible for someone to meet every event of his or her life with a question.

"What would I do in this situation if I acted like I believed the Bible was true?"

That simple idea began a life of decisions, guided by the still whispers within me. I would love to tell you that I always acted like I believed the Bible was true. I can't.

Yet, even in those times when I didn't, there was always a quiet voice within, calling me back to this idea.

Over the decades, the idea became second-nature. It produced enough benefit that it would amaze me when others refused to try it. They could intellectually acknowledge that it seemed like a good idea, but they wouldn't put it into consistent practice.

And then there were those around me who seemed intent on self-destruction. They were intelligent individuals who loved God. Yet, they engaged in behaviors that they knew were bad for their bodies, bad for their emotions and/or bad for their minds.

Of course, the Christian belief system identifies this conflict as a struggle between the flesh and the spirit. Many other belief systems recognize this duality as well.

If you spend any time watching humans you will quickly see behavior that can only be described as foolish.

What I couldn't comprehend was this: If these destructive behaviors were driven by the "flesh"—or by some kind of animal instinct, if you prefer that term—what was the ultimate benefit to the flesh? How were the behaviors "successful" for the flesh? And if they weren't, why would the flesh inspire such behavior?

(At the time, when attempting to understand any person's behavior, I would ask myself, "How is this successful for the person?")

Unfortunately, there were many behaviors that I simply couldn't explain. Behaviors that seemed unquestionably toxic. This conundrum set the stage for the second pivot point of my life.

I'm not sure when it happened but it was close to the turn of the millennium. I was out for my morning run, pondering self-destruction once again, trying to figure out how life worked, trying to sort out the motives on the flesh.

I was mulling it over, *yet again*, half praying, half talking to myself, half grousing about the fact that it didn't make any sense.

"It makes perfect sense," a whisper chided, "if you understand that their flesh hates them."

The idea startled me. I took a moment to absorb it before all the ill-fitting pieces of human behavior suddenly locked into place.

I spent the rest of the run testing the whisper against everything I had observed for the past forty years. By the time I returned home I had a framework that defined all of human behavior in simple, usable terms. A framework that would allow me to live every moment of every day knowing that the decisions that I made would be the right decisions and they would create around me an environment of success.

It was an amazing day that changed my life.

the framework

"It makes perfect sense if you understand that their flesh hates them."

Until that moment, I had always thought of my "flesh" in the same way I thought of my body. It was a part of me. It was like an inner child that didn't really understand the consequences of what it wanted. It just "wanted": more food, more entertainment, more sex, more fun, less work, less stress, less responsibility, less "bother."

Until that moment, my standard approach in dealing with my flesh was to remind myself that I was an adult, not a child and simply trying to get whatever I "wanted" was not a long term strategy of success.

This idea of my flesh hating me changed everything. No longer was the flesh a collection of "wants." If the flesh could hate, the flesh was more than urges. It was a conscious entity within me. And if it hated me, it was dedicated to my destruction.

This simple idea clarified my entire approach to life because it spawned what I eventually — and unimaginatively — called the "framework."

The framework is a simple series of statements:

Within me there are two opposing entities: flesh and spirit.

The flesh hates me and wants me to fail.

The spirit loves me and wants me to succeed.

The flesh is a liar and will use every deceit and treachery that it can conceive.

The spirit always speaks truth and that truth represents my freedom.

When I share this with friends over dinner, I often grab a napkin (i.e. a serviette for those of you who speak proper English) and draw a line down the middle. I title the left half "flesh" and the right half "spirit." Underneath these two headings I begin to write individual words, moving back and forth between the two areas:

"Condemnation, Mercy;

"Hate, Love;

"Greed, Kindness;

"Envy, Generosity;

"Isolation, Community…"

It only takes two or three pairs before everyone gets the concept. All the wonderful things in life are spirit. All the terrible things are flesh. If we take the time to consider our thoughts and words, our emotions and actions, we can usually determine what comes from flesh and what comes from spirit.

And that's the central truth of the framework, *everything* that proceeds out of your life, every thought, every word, every emotion and every action, *everything*, comes from flesh or spirit.

If it originates from your flesh, it is designed to lead you closer to failure in some way. If it originates from your spirit, it is designed to lead you closer to success in some way.

What becomes vitally important then is for us to choose the thoughts, words, emotions and actions that are inspired by our spirit because over time those choices will inevitably lead us to success.

(You may be thinking at this point, "Wait a minute. How can I 'choose' an emotion? Emotions just happen. How am I not supposed to feel something?"

In fact, you can choose your emotions, just like you can choose your words and actions. The illusion that you can't is manufactured by your flesh to persuade you that your emotions—and thoughts—are beyond your control. If your flesh can convince you of this simple lie, it has a tool to twist your life towards turmoil…but that is a topic for another chapter.)

Achieving a life of abundance in Christ is as simple as knowing his voice, hearing him call you by name, and following him.

Every day.

Your main obstacle to this effort will be the cacophony that your flesh generates to keep you from this goal (or to confuse you into thinking that you are heading towards this goal when, in fact, you are being led away from it). It would be wonderful if we could just erase the flesh from our lives. Unfortunately, that doesn't seem possible.

What *is* possible, is "noise reduction." I have a collection of actions, approaches and analogies to turn down the volume on the voices that seek my failure.

Reducing the noise helps me hear more clearly, and recognize more readily, the voice of the Great Shepherd.

The result is abundance.

You can read the following chapters in any order. I've tried to organize them in a mixture of topics, viewpoints and lengths to keep the book interesting.

There will be times when I will repeat myself. I've found that it helps me to cover the same material from a variety of angles.

If a given chapter doesn't seem appropriate to your situation, skip it and return to it later. During my dinners with friends, we never cover everything at once. We work our way forward, listening for direction.

Unfortunately, books aren't capable of that kind of interaction so you will need to provide your own guidance on the topics that are current in your life. And you will need to supply your own pacing. You won't find much use for the information here if you simply give it a cursory read and then never return to dwell on it. It takes time to move these concepts from your awareness to your knowledge to your experience. That why I use the term "meditations" in the subtitle of this book. These are things that you need to think about as you are moving through your day.

To the quest then…

To the clearing of the atmosphere of your life…

To abundance.

genesis

Every thought, every emotion, every word and every action begins in the same place. Each of them begins with a belief.

Take, for example, the man who is driving on a city street when another driver cuts him off. Instantly, the man is angry. Perhaps, he honks his horn. Perhaps he shakes his fist or shouts obscenities.

If you ask the man why he is angry, he will say it is because the other driver cut him off.

This is a lie.

The man's anger is not caused by the action of the other driver. The man's anger is caused by his own beliefs.

The man believes that the other driver cut him off on purpose. The man believes the other driver is showing him disrespect. But mostly, the man believes that he is more important than anyone else on the road and everyone else should figure that out and get out of his way.

All these beliefs exist at the man's core because his flesh has spawned them and the man has accepted them.

But the truth is much different. The truth is that the man is not more important than everyone else. The truth is that the other driver may have not seen the man. Perhaps the other driver had just received word that his spouse is on the way to the hospital and the other driver is distracted with concern. There are many possible explanations for the other driver's actions and few of them carry any malice.

Yet, the man has instantly consumed the explanation that fuels his greatest anger because that belief was specifically chosen by his flesh to make him angry.

If the man pauses for a moment to consider the situation, he might realize there are other explanations. He might hear the spirit reminding him that he is not the only person who has a right to be on the road.

And his emotion will change.

The key to choosing the thoughts, emotions, words and actions that you exhibit lies in this understanding. Every thought, every emotion, every word and every action carries a belief. If you take the time to examine those beliefs, you will quickly be able to determine if they come from your flesh or your spirit.

Many months ago, I sat across the table from a professor. After we had discussed these ideas for a few moments, he asked me to comment on a situation he had recently encountered.

He recalled the story of a young man and his wife who were seeking to serve as youth ministers. Suddenly, what seemed like the ideal position became available. They interviewed for the position. They prayed about it and eventually accepted.

A short time later, the professor saw the young man. The professor could see the distress in the young man's face. He quickly agreed to meet.

As they conversed, the young man said that he now believed that he had made a terrible mistake, that he shouldn't have accepted the position. The professor asked the young man what his wife thought. The young man responded that his wife thought he was crazy. But, the young man couldn't shake the feeling that he shouldn't go to work for the church.

After relating this story, the professor looked at me and asked, "Was that flesh or spirit?"

I smiled. Once you understand the active, destructive nature of the flesh and how it influences us, it is quite simple to ferret out its attempts. All you have to do is pause and asked yourself which lie the flesh is attempting to peddle. (And, yes, there are a limited number of them.)

I replied, "So, in other words, this young man believes that when he was praying for guidance in this situation, God was reading a newspaper and only after the young man made the decision did God look up and exclaim, 'Rats! I should have been paying closer attention. I guess I really missed the boat on that one.'"

Obviously, I'm being silly. But if this young man would have simply acted like he believed the Bible, he would have never subjected himself to distress. He would have reminded himself that Jesus told us that God will not give us a stone when we ask for bread.

Instead, the young man allowed himself to be fooled into believing that God had failed him; that God was not capable of communicating with him and perhaps even that God had abandoned him.

No wonder he felt such distress.

And, it was obviously caused by his flesh.

this body of DEATH

In Romans chapter 7, the Apostle Paul makes a series of anguished observations regarding his struggle with his sin nature (i.e. his flesh). They culminate in verse 24 with:

"What a wretched man I am! Who will rescue me from this body of death?" (NIV)

While I have been unable to confirm one interpretation of this verse, the analogy is so powerful and useful that I wanted to share it with you.

Some commentators believe that the phrase "body of death" refers to an ancient punishment. Supposedly, this ancient punishment involved chaining a murderer to his victim in such a way that the murderer would have to carry the corpse with him wherever he went. Eventually the corruption of the putrefying corpse would spread to the murderer and extinguish his life.

I have found that it helps me to think of the flesh in this way, as a "body of death" that was once draped over me, it's decaying head nestled against my shoulder, it's croaking voice mere inches from my ear.

In speaking with frustrated husbands, I often use this analogy to defuse the pent up emotions that they harbor against their wives. I usually give them some opportunity to rehearse the litany of wounds they carry from their wives' behavior but eventually I raise my hand and share this analogy with them.

I point out that they carry this body of death with them and the very first step is for them to find freedom from it.

I then observe that their wives are bound to these bodies of death as well.

I continue with, "I know your wife has done things that have hurt you. But what if another force is at work within her, prompting her, deceiving her? What if you could look at your beloved and could see this body of death clinging to her, whispering in her ear with its maggot-encrusted lips? What if you could look at your beloved and could see the confusion in her eyes? Would you still be hurt and angry over her actions? Or would you simply wish to do everything you could to help free her from her torture?"

Invariably, the husband nods and compassion rises in his eyes.

This is another example of how the beliefs that we embrace fuel our thoughts and emotions. Once the husband understands that the behavior which seems intentionally designed to frustrate him (because it is) does not come from his wife but from the "body of death," he can dismiss the notion that his wife is the enemy.

The analogy is useful on a larger scale as well. We should always remember that every human being carries the "God-breath" — every human being carries the spark of the Divine. But every human being also carries, in some fashion, the body of death.

This body of death is the first of the two main sources of evil in the world and its sole purpose is to kill, steal and destroy in every way and in any way that it can.

He STANDS in the future

Several years ago, my wife and I decided to finish the basement of our house. Until then, I had found the unfinished basement very convenient.

I love electronics. Because of the layout of our house, it was better to put the television on one wall of the living room and all the audio-visual equipment on another. Of course, that meant that I had to run wires but that wasn't really a problem because...I had an unfinished basement!

However, I knew that once I finished the basement, I was going to lose my access unless I did some fancy planning. So, I mapped out my options and determined that the best approach would be to put floor boxes in my living room so I could run cabling as needed. I was able to get one of the floor boxes for free. That left one more.

Unfortunately, because of the way the floor joists run in my house I needed a box that was a specific size (long and narrow).

I called a local music equipment store. They had a box. It was a bit expensive but it met the requirements and the measurements seemed right so I bought it. As I recall, it was the last one they had.

That evening as I was preparing to install it, I realized that when I measured the box, I measured the bottom of the box. The top of the box had a lip that stuck out one inch all the way around. That extra inch meant that I couldn't get close enough to the wall to fit the box between the floor joists.

In other words, the box was not going to work where I had planned to install it. At this point, it would have been easy to stomp around and yell at myself for being stupid and kick the floor box around the room.

However, I had been mulling a phrase for weeks and it offered a much better approach. For weeks, I had reminded myself, my daughter and her boyfriend—who was helping us finish the basement—that:

"He stands in the future." (Jesus, that is, not the boyfriend.)

Obviously, if Jesus stood in the future, he already knew the box wasn't going to fit. And if he already knew that it wouldn't fit, he had already provided a solution of some sort. I just needed to find it.

After mentioning to my daughter and her boyfriend that the box wasn't going to fit, I trundled downstairs and started looking for the solution that Jesus had already provided.

As it turned out, the main support beam for the first floor of my house was located four or five feet from the spot I had picked for the second floor box.

And, it just so happened, that the Amish carpenters who framed my house overlapped the floor joists at that support beam.

And they just happened to overlap them in the perfect way to give me an extra inch and a half of wiggle room where the floor joists crossed the support beam.

I marked the location. I went upstairs. My father-in-law wielded his reciprocating saw. We tried the box. It was a little tight. A couple more zips with the saw. And...

I drop the box in place and it looked like it was designed to go there from the beginning.

This is when I looked at my daughter and boyfriend and smiled.

"He stands in the future," I said, "Years ago, when the Amish were framing this house they had a choice and Jesus whispered to them to stagger the floor joists in a particular way. Months ago, when the local professional audio shop ordered floor boxes they had lots of options but Jesus whispered to them and they ordered a particular box with a particular set of dimensions. That meant that when I needed a floor box, the one floor box that I needed was already sitting in the inventory of the local professional audio shop and my floor joists were already in the exact configuration for that specific floor box because...he stands in the future."

In the weeks that followed, I added to the saying a bit.

You might find it useful.

He stands in the future. We are all toddlers learning to walk in Eternity. But, he stands in the future, with his arms stretched towards us, whispering sweet words of encouragement.

the carnal AGE

What is the age of the carnal nature?

The question may seem odd but the answer is useful.

The carnal nature (i.e. the flesh)…is twelve.

If you hear yourself talking like a twelve year old, that's the flesh. If you find yourself wishing that you were twelve again, that's the flesh.

If your emotions are thrashing back and forth;

If you're in a situation that feels like junior high;

If there's pouting;

If there's drama;

If there's stomping;

If eyes are rolling and noses are snorting…

There's flesh involved.

And where there's flesh…eventually, there's failure.

coherence

I've always found science fascinating. I almost chose it for my career but music called me on a deeper level. Still, I am always interested in hearing about the latest exploration and theories...especially in the field of physics.

I remember the first time I heard about the "big bang" — the theory that gives the universe a definite beginning as opposed to some kind of "steady-state" existence.

I smiled.

Because, of course, the Bible says that the universe had a beginning.

I've been even more fascinated by the advance of the theories of quantum mechanics. I won't try to pretend that I understand them or can even approach the math involved. (I've always loved math as well but my life took a different journey.)

Yet, the more information that I pick up trickling down to the masses from the quantum mechanics community, the more it sounds strangely familiar.

In quantum mechanics, particles can have "superposition" (i.e. they can be in two places at once). Particles can also be "entangled." No matter what the distance between these particles, a change in one is immediately reflected in the other. Particles can move through time as easily as they move through space.

In addition, the theorists say that the quantum world is filled with an energy field, an energy field that is all present and close enough to be called all powerful.

In short, the quantum world sounds a lot like the characteristics we ascribe to the Divine: all present, all knowing, all powerful.

How interesting that when we look in our own basement we find eternity seeping upward.

But actually…"basement" isn't the most descriptive term because it implies a downward direction. If the theorists are correct, *everything* in our existence rises out of quantum realm, from the stars in the sky to the air that you breathe to the molten core of planet Earth. Every single unit of the reality that we perceive is indivisibly connected to the quantum realm.

So why don't we see the mind-warping aspects of the quantum realm interrupting our daily lives? Why do we perceive objects in only one location? Why do we live in a procession of time with past, present and future?

Because something odd happens when information transitions out of the quantum realm, it coalesces and forms what we call reality. And as far as I've been able to tell, none of the theorists know exactly how or why this happens.

With that as a background, listen to the Apostle Paul's statements about Jesus Christ in the first chapter of Colossians,

"He is the image of the invisible God, the firstborn over all creation. For by him all things were created: things in heaven and on earth, visible and invisible, whether thrones or powers or rulers or authorities; all things were created by him and for him. He is before all things, and in him all things hold together." (Colossians 1:16-17 NIV)

That last phrase can be translated a number of different ways.

"...in him all things are placed together."

"...in him all things band together."

"...in him all things *cohere*."

If this means what I think it means and the theory of quantum mechanics is correct, Jesus is actively managing a boundary in Eternity and using that boundary to create a reality for us.

Every oxygen molecule that you breathe is held together by Christ.

Every drop of water that you drink is held together by Christ.

Every thought that you think is processed through neurons that exist solely because Christ is willing them to exist.

(I'll let you supply the rest of the "everys.")

And he's performing this management in every unit of reality across a universe that is billions and billions of light-years across.

Given this, it isn't hard to imagine what the Bible means when it assigns the Divine the qualities of being all powerful, all present and all knowing.

After all, if the Divine coheres the very atoms that compose the hairs on your head, he probably knows how many there are at any given moment...which is exactly what Jesus claimed.

(A side note: For those of you who are more familiar with quantum mechanics, it might be interesting to ponder the role of Jesus as the Observer who collapses the wave function and then consider how this integrates with the concepts of foreknowledge and predestination.)

the glory of **KINGS**

I highly recommend reading *The Privileged Planet*. It is a book that beautifully illustrates Proverbs 25:2 (NIV), "It is the glory of God to conceal a matter; to search out a matter is the glory of kings."

The Divine made this world for us. He stuffed it full of mysteries and every time we uncover one of them I'm convinced he smiles and thinks, "Good job!"

I remember watching a video of the last moments before one of the rovers touched Martian soil. Because of the entry into Mars' atmosphere, all radio contact was lost. Everyone in the mission control room grew quiet.

Waiting. Waiting. Waiting. Not sure if the rover had survived entry.

Waiting.

And then someone in the room proclaimed radio contact and everyone cheered. NASA had hurled a small go-cart tens of millions of miles through space and it was sitting on a neighboring planet, sending back snapshots.

"Good job!" God cheered right along with them.

Over and over with every triumph of science.

"Good job!"

Yes, I know that many of these scientists are absolutely opposed to the concept of a Designer.

But, the Eternal knows that this is just confusion brought on by their flesh. We're his children. He loves us. He crafted for us this great adventure and placed far more wonders in our existence than we will ever uncover.

For instance, it may be common knowledge by the time you read this book, but just today (October 22, 2008) I read an article about UCLA scientists who are experimenting with a surprising method for producing X-rays.

Turns out that if you peel Scotch tape off a roll and you do it in a vacuum chamber, it produces X-rays! This is not a joke. It really does! The scientists are postulating that they could create a portable inexpensive X-ray machine from this that could be human-powered with a crank.

How fabulous is that?

Every answer we need is already here.

We just have to seek them out.

painting DAISIES

If it is true that the truth will set you free, it is also true that lies will bind you.

This is why it is so important to guard your words. If I ever have the opportunity to work with you on a project, you will soon notice an affectation in my speech patterns. At times, I will say something, pause, and then state it again in a manner that more correctly communicates what I am trying to say. And sometimes, the corrections will sound trivial.

After hearing this a few times, you might conclude that I am being overly cautious—that I am being guarded lest I be misconstrued. But I don't do this because I'm afraid. I do this because I am attempting to speak the truth and sometimes after I utter a sentence, the Divine will whisper that the words I've just spoken did not effectively communicate truth.

And so, to honor those I speak with and to honor the Divine within me, I rephrase.

Too often, human are loose with their words.

For instance, an individual bustles in, late for a meeting.

"I would have been here on time but I got behind this guy who was driving ten miles an hour under the speed limit!"

In other words, the individual has taken a lie (i.e. that the reason that he or she is late is someone else's fault)...

Painted daisies on it...

And has tried to pass it off as an excuse.

Everyone in the room nods politely and the individual feels justified. There's no need to change any behavior; no need to leave five minutes early instead of the very last minute. Because, in the future, all the traffic will magically flow exactly as needed to put the individual at his or her appointment on time.

And if it doesn't? That isn't a problem either because it will be someone's fault that the individual was late.

Consequently, the individual never changes his or her behavior. The lie—even when it is decorated as an excuse—remains a lie and binds the individual to repeat the behavior.

Even more interesting, the individual cannot see the lie for what it is because he or she becomes enamored with his or her artwork. He or she will actually begin to believe that his or her lateness is always someone else's fault.

At the same time, everyone else will start noticing a pattern to the individual's lateness. They will conclude that the individual's lateness is not the "occasional and unavoidable" kind but rather the "my time is more important to me than your time" kind.

If the individual is very fortunate, he or she will have an employer who will intervene in the matter and attempt to administer truth. If not, the individual will continue painting daisies, fooling no one but themselves.

It is far better to abandon this kind of artwork and simply speak the truth:

"I apologize for being late. I didn't plan my time very well this morning. I will attempt to do better in the future."

 suicide

I have a trick that I often employ when I'm dealing with my flesh. I engage in a form of suicide.

Here's the problem: if you struggle against the flesh you just get stinky because you're wrestling with a rotting corpse. (See the chapter, "This Body of Death.") And besides, the more the flesh has your attention, the easier it is to communicate with you.

Instead of engaging the flesh in combat, I first try to treat it like it's dead. If that doesn't work, I do my best to drive a stake through its heart by doing the opposite of what it suggests.

For instance, we recently hosted a dinner at our house for my mom's birthday. As part of my effort to help, I set the table (with all the dishes, glasses and attending silverware). Then my wife asked me to dust the furniture and I happily trundled around the dining area with the duster trying my best to do a good job.

At one point, I looked up and decided to tackle the ceiling fan. So I pulled out the extension to the duster and went to work…and promptly produced a "rain" of dust that settle over a third of the table.

At first I took my flesh's suggestion that I should just get a paper towel and flick off the dust and no one would be the wiser. But as I was conducting this bit of subterfuge, the flesh kept pushing its agenda:

"There, see, that's better. No one will ever know that you knocked dust over everything. Besides a little dust isn't going to hurt anyone. And no one will know, so there's no problem. It looks great. And it's sure a lot better than setting all those plates. And if you reset the plates, you're going to have to admit that you knocked dust all over everything and then…"

Somewhere around this point, I was finished listening because I knew my flesh wasn't going to pipe down any time soon so I picked the action that would completely take away any opportunity for it to continue its prattle.

I walked into the kitchen, told my wife what had happened and pulled out enough plates, glasses, silverware and napkins to reset the affected portion of the table.

And the noise level dropped within me.

I use the same technique in my consulting work. When I discover that I have made a mistake and there's data that needs to be fixed, my flesh will suggest that I just fix the data and hide the time in another task.

As soon as I hear that, I get up from desk walk over to whomever I'm reporting to, tell him or her about it, come back, fix the data, and document that I have fixed the data in my time sheets.

This puts an immediate end to the discussion.

It puts that effort of the flesh to death and it allows me to move on.

Remember that whatever your flesh is suggesting, it is suggesting it to create an environment of failure. Most of the time, if you do exactly what your flesh *doesn't* want you to do, you'll create an environment of success.

GOD on trial

It happens every time there's a major tragedy.

The 9/11 attack on the World Trade Center in New York City; The I-35W bridge collapse in Minneapolis on August 1, 2007; the death of a spouse; any other catastrophe vast or narrow.

No matter where we are when we see these things happen to others or when we experience them first-hand, the flesh within us trots out its portable courtroom and puts God on trial.

It casts itself in the role of the prosecuting attorney and makes the case:

"Where was God? Why did let this happen? If he really is a God of love, how can he allow such suffering in the world?"

Assuming the role of the judge, the flesh then instructs the jury to reach a verdict. And, being the only member on the jury, it quickly finds the Divine guilty of neglect and makes the impassionate plea for us to reject him.

Of course, the flesh completely ignores the news stories that are written days, weeks and months later — the articles that indicate there were hints that we ignored and clues that we missed.

"Could It Have Been Prevented?" the headline asks. Often, the answer is "yes."

There isn't enough space or time in this chapter to exhaustively review every recent mass tragedy or even all that is now known about the events leading up to the destruction of the World Trade Center on September 11, 2001. But listen to the words of the Director of National Intelligence, Michael McConnell in 2007 when addressing members of the House Judiciary Committee.

He admitted, "9/11 should have and could have been prevented." He then added, "It was an issue of connecting information that was available."

In other words, there were those involved in the security agencies in the United States who had noted suspicious behaviors but those observations were discarded.

The following information comes from the official 9/11 Commission Report:

In July of 2001, an FBI field agent in the Phoenix, Arizona office drafts a memo to FBI headquarters advising the "possibility of a coordinated effort by Usama Bin Ladin" to send students to flight school. This agent bases his theory on the "inordinate number of individuals of investigative interest" who are attending these schools in Arizona. The memo urges a nationwide survey of other civil aviation schools to determine if the same is happening elsewhere.

A month later, Zaccarias Moussouai is detained by the FBI in Minneapolis, Minnesota. Instructors at the Pan Am International Flight Academy in Eagan, Minnesota have tagged Moussouai as suspicious. Through interrogation, an FBI field agent soon learns that Moussouai holds jihadist beliefs and that Moussouai has $32,000 in a bank account that he can't explain. This agent concludes that Moussouai is "an Islamic extremist preparing for some future act in furtherance of radical fundamentalist goals." And the agent believes that these goals are related to his flight training.

The Minneapolis FBI office wishes to investigate further and seeks a special warrant under the Foreign Intelligence Surveillance Act (FISA). In order for the warrant to be granted, a belief must be justified that Moussouai is an agent of a foreign power and engaged in espionage or terrorism. This leads to a series of inter-agency information requests and discussions. The official 9/11 Commission Report notes that if a nationwide survey had been underway as a result of the Arizona field office memo, the Moussouai investigation might have been given more serious attention.

Instead, there was *substantial* disagreement between the Minneapolis field office and FBI headquarters.

At one point, the Minneapolis supervisor is even chastised by an individual at FBI headquarters because the supervisor's FISA request was "couched in a manner intended to get people 'spun up.'" The Minneapolis supervisor readily agrees that this was his intent. He even tells the headquarters agent that he is...

..."trying to keep someone from taking a plane and crashing into the World Trade Center."

Upon hearing this, the headquarters agent replies that this wasn't going to happen because Zaccarias Moussouai wasn't a terrorist. (Zaccarias Moussouai later becomes the only individual put on trial for the terrorist attack on the World Trade Center in 2001.)

In other words, the idea that someone could fly an airplane into the World Trade Center seized an FBI supervisor in Minneapolis mere weeks before it actually occurred.

Moving backwards in time we see the trail of hints and nudges that lead to this moment. When a Minneapolis agent is interrogating Zaccarias Moussouai, some intuition within him is flashing red. When Zaccarias Moussouai arrives at the Pan Am International Flight Academy in Eagan, Minnesota, a feeling bubbles up in the flight instructors who teach there. They know. Something is wrong with the situation.

Of course, there comes a point when the Minneapolis field agents need to file for a FISA special warrant. And, the elements that *should* give that request a high priority are already in play because the same intuitions, the same feelings have disturbed a set of flight instructors and FBI agents at the opposite edge of the United States in Phoenix, Arizona.

But those elements don't give the FISA request any priority because they are never implemented and the FISA warrant isn't issued in time.

Why?

Did God fail?

Hardly, he was working at every step, whispering, suggesting, and providing every opportunity to turn the outcome.

But...along the line...someone's flesh or a "whole lotta flesh" buried that opportunity. I'm not suggesting it was a coordinated effort on the part of the flesh (although that is a topic for another chapter). I'm suggesting that somewhere along the line someone had an argument with a spouse, or a hangover, or a flat tire, or a bad stock pick...

And when the critical piece of information came across his or her desk there was so much noise in his or her system that he or she brushed it aside.

So where was God during the destruction of the World Trade Center? Why didn't he prevent it from happening?

He tried. He tried in a number of ways that we recognize and in thousands of ways that we don't.

And we ignored him, just like we do in many, many tragedies.

I firmly believe that when all is known about this life, we will see that much of the evil that has occurred in this world could have been prevented if we had just listened.

"Well, then, God should talk louder," the flesh accuses.

But the flesh already knows that God won't do this. The Eternal made this planet for us. He gave it to us and provided us with free will. If he shouted at us, we *might* do what he says but not because we chose to do it. We would do it because a voice suddenly began booming out of the walls of our offices.

So when the flesh trots out its courtroom, remember that the prosecuting attorney, judge and jury probably bear far more responsibility than the one being accused.

On the other hand, I realize that there are certain tragedies that are simply acts of nature and no amount of listening would keep the event from occurring.

But if we are honest, we will be forced to admit that— even in these situations—listening and awareness could certainly affect the death toll.

Consider the December 26th, 2004 tsunami. While some had no inkling that a tidal wave would soon engulf them, others knew what to look for and acted on that knowledge.

The oral tradition of those native to the Indonesian island of Simeulue contains references to a 1907 tsunami. In 2004, when the islanders saw a receding tide following the earthquake, they recognized it as a sign that the tsunami was coming. They evacuated to higher ground, thereby surviving the massive wall of water.

In fact, a presentation to the American Geophysical Union indicated that a tsunami which struck Papua New Guinea in 1930 with similar intensity resulted in only a fraction of the deaths attributed to the 2004 tsunami and the researchers attributed this to the oral traditions of the local inhabitants that allowed the local inhabitants to recognize the warning signs and seek refuge inland.

I note this simply to help us recognize that the impact of tragedies can be magnified by a loss of communication and community.

God will not force us to repair our isolation. Our choice of isolation is directly related to our free will.

God is not the engine of tragedy in the world and even when he allows tragedy to overtake us it is not from a lack of love.

As an act of love, God created this planet for us. As an act of love, God gave us the ability to choose our own path in life, to live our own epic, to forge our own adventure, to bear the consequences of our choices. And as an act of love, he whispers to us every day seeking to create an environment of success for us, giving us advice, comfort and words of encouragement.

But he will never force us to take them.

So, whenever you hear your flesh put God on trial, stop and get quiet. Take time to consider if the tragedy is of your own doing.

If it is, admit this and know that—while there may be consequences—the Divine will certainly help you through it.

And if you determine that the tragedy is not your own doing and you were faithful to consider his voice in the days prior to it, then pay attention to where the tragedy leads you because God has a specific purpose for you there.

Many years ago, I watched a special on PBS that explored the effect of television on children. In one scene, an interviewer asked a collection of elementary students if they thought the stories they saw on television were real.

All answered with a resounding, "No." They assured the interviewer that the stories on television were just make-believe.

As I recall, the interviewer went through a few more topics and then asked the children what the executive board room for a big company looked like.

The children were quick to answer: Big wooden table, leather chairs, wood paneling, etc.

Smiling, the interviewer asked the children how many of them had ever visited an executive board room for a big company.

No one raised a hand.

Where did the children develop this "knowledge" of what an executive boardroom looked like? From television and the movies, of course.

Yet, they were as certain as they could be that the image was true.

We carry many of these "certainties" with us.

What does a prostitute look like? She's beautiful and shapely, of course. (Until you see one of the $50 streetwalkers on news footage and then...not so much.)

What happens when people get together and consume large amounts of alcohol? Everyone has a rollicking time. (Except for the women who get raped after they pass out.)

And we all know that every pregnant teenage girl is plucky and erudite...

And every dad is a goof-ball...

And every mom has to be the sole grown-up for the entire family...

And every teenager...

You get the picture...literally.

Because while you may dismiss the entertainment you watch as just stories, the images that form the structure around the story are slipping past your analytical grid and forming memories that are indistinguishable from the memories that you form as you live your life.

For five years, I actually made my living running a subversive scheme to reduce the effectiveness of this mechanism. I wrote a series of books called Nitpicker's Guides.

I would spend months watching a chosen science fiction television series (*Star Trek*; *Star Trek: the Next Generation*; *Star Trek: Deep Space Nine*; *The X-Files*). I would then compile lists of plot oversights, changed premises, equipment oddities and continuity and production problems.

Things like:

The moment in the *Star Trek: the Next Generation* episode "Half a Life," when a character walks in front of a mirror and you can see the reflection of a boom microphone dipping into the shot.

Or, the moment in *The X-Files* episode "The Blessing Way" when the hallway outside Fox Mulder's apartment is five or six feet shorter than it is in episodes before and after it.

I put out five Nitpicker's Guides over those five years and a "good time was had by all." They were fun and light-hearted and it gave my cadre of nitpickers a chance to peek behind the production curtain and remember that it really *was* just make believe.

Over time, I received 10,000 letters from my readers. My favorites were the ones that started with something like, "What have you done to me?! I used to be able to just sit and watch television and now I'm always looking for nits."

Of course, that was a small part of the plan all along. It was my little subversive way to get viewers to be more active in their viewing. And it certainly seemed to work. It even garnered me a small bit of "fifteen minute" fame in the Trekker community.

But, it certainly didn't make me very popular with the creators of the series. As was my custom at Star Trek conventions, I once asked one of the speakers—an assistant to an executive producer—to sign a personal copy of one of my guides. When I identified myself as the author, he shot me a look that should have sent a dagger through my heart.

I just laughed and said, "Oh, come on. It's all in fun. Sign my book!"

He did, writing, "Phil, Quit it! We're trying!"

And try they do! Their livelihood is dependent on the number of eyeballs that they can keep focused on their programs.

If they need to put "pretty" on the screen to keep your eyeballs glued, they'll do it (and use whatever costumes they think they can get away with).

If they need to put "violent" on the screen, they'll do that too.

Their goal is to be "shiny," not accurate.

That's why every time my family and I watch a movie that's "based on real life" we immediately go to the internet afterwards to find out what is historically accurate and what isn't.

For me, though, one of the most intriguing developments in the area of image creation by the media is the rise of the contracted "photoshoppers."

For those of you who may not be aware Adobe Photoshop is the premiere image manipulation software application. The range of tools available in the program for altering photographs is nothing short of amazing.

Of course, image manipulation has been going on in the media for some time. You might recall the movie poster for Julia Roberts' break out movie *Pretty Woman*. It features Richard Gere in a black suit back-to-back with Julia Roberts who is dressed in an ensemble that features a mini-dress with a tight pink top and black body-hugging micro-skirt...and thigh-high black vinyl stiletto boots.

Except, the creators apparently didn't believe that Julia Roberts (as she was then) cut the right figure so they hired a body double for the actual shoot and then replaced the head of the body double with a photograph of Julia Roberts.

These days, there's no need to hire the extra person.

An image manipulation program in the hands of a talented artist can do almost anything. Lips not plump enough? No problem. Neck not long enough? No problem.

Breasts too small? Waist too thick? Facial imperfections? Cellulite? Knobby knees? Wrong color eyes? Stained teeth? Need to lose ten pounds?

No problem. No problem. No problem. No problem. No problem. No problem. No problem.

In fact, the word on the street is that major female actors have professional "photoshoppers" under contract to review each image that's going to be released to make sure that it has the appropriate modifications that will show the actor in the best possible light.

This is sad. These are some of the most beautiful women in the world but it's not good enough, they feel they have to be more "shiny" than they are.

We could spend an entire chapter talking about how the flesh uses this to grind women and men with unreal expectations but that's not the point of this chapter.

The point of this chapter is to remind you that nothing you see in the visual mass medium happens accidentally and most of it has been manipulated in some manner to make it more engaging. If you blindly accept the images, you are blindly accepting lies in your storehouse of memories and eventually the weight of those images will skew your worldview.

Instead, question every image and remind yourself that what you are seeing is not real and it doesn't deserve your prolonged attention.

JESUS on the sandlot

There's a fascinating exchange early in the book of Joshua. The Israelites have crossed over the Jordan River. They are preparing to march on the city of Jericho. God has told them that the land of Palestine belongs to them and they should take it by force.

As Joshua nears Jericho, he looks up and sees a man standing before him with a drawn sword.

Understandably enough, Joshua asks, "Are you for us or for our enemies?"

And the "man" who later identifies himself as the commander of the army of the Lord...

...the "man" who is most probably an early manifestation of Jesus (Theologians call this a "Christophany")...

...the "man" who is intimately connected with the same God that has told Joshua to possess the land of Palestine...

...the "man" when asked if he is for the Israelites or for the inhabitants of Palestine...

...*this* man answers...

"Neither."

Neither?

Neither?!

Isn't God supposed to be for the Israelites—his chosen people—and against everyone else?

After all, he recruited Abraham, not the other way around.

It's almost like Jesus built Abraham's team, primed them for the game, coached them, made sure they were ready and led them to another neighborhood's sandlot.

Everyone sizes up everyone else. Abraham wins the chance to pick first and he does exactly what any good captain would do.

He says, "I'll take Jesus."

And Jesus says, "Nope."

Nervously, Abraham picks someone else and waits for the other captain to pick. Of course, the other captain picks Jesus as well.

"Nope," Jesus responds a second time.

Back and forth it goes. In every round, each captain tries to get Jesus to commit to one of the teams.

But Jesus keeps saying, "Nope."

Finally, only Jesus remains to be chosen. The captains look at each other and then at Jesus.

"So whose team are you going to be on?" they asked, exasperated.

"I'm not on either of your teams," Jesus replies, "You're on mine. Now, go play ball."

That simple word, "neither," tells us so much about our relationships with other humans.

Don't ever allow your flesh to draw a line in your mind to separate "us" from "them" — be it African-American versus Caucasian versus Asian versus Latino; or male versus female; or Mormon versus Buddhist; or Baptist versus Charismatic; or homosexual versus heterosexual versus transsexual; or red state versus blue state; or rich versus poor.

The Apostle Paul, in Galatians 3:28, tells us that in Jesus Christ there is no Jew or Greek, slave or free, male or female.

There is only one thing you guarantee when you draw a circle around yourself to shut out the rest of humanity.

You guarantee that Jesus will be standing outside of your circle whispering for you to join him.

So, why is it so satisfying to mark other humans as the enemy? Because every time you do, your flesh will pat you on the back and say, "Oh, you are so wise to comprehend this difference!"

It knows that if you are busy focusing outward on a false enemy, you won't be focusing inward on the real enemy.

One final item before we move on. You might be thinking, "Wait a minute, this doesn't make any sense. God told Joshua to conquer Palestine (and that conquering included a lot of killing). It doesn't matter what the commander of the army of the Lord said...God sided with the Israelites."

And that would be your flesh talking.

Here's reality: Not only is God not on your team, he doesn't play by your rules. And he doesn't have to order his conduct so that his actions "make sense" to you.

un⌒church

Several years ago, my wife and I travelled to Vancouver, British Columbia in Canada. That Sunday, we took the ferry to Victoria on Vancouver Island.

It was a gorgeous day. We did some sight-seeing and walked down to the ocean front. There were street performers, sailboats in slips along the water's edge, vendors selling a little of this and a little of that.

Everyone seemed to be enjoying the peaceful, pleasant morning.

At one point, I looked at my wife and asked, "Why would any of these people want to be in church?"

(Now, before you get offended, remember that the name of this chapter is "Un-Church" not "Anti-Church." Keep reading.)

For many years, there has been dissatisfaction within me over the standard practices of mainline Christianity. While I recognize that truth is not measured by results, I am pragmatic enough to believe that truth should have some positive effect on our lives. Yet, when I look at the organized church in America, I see:

Couples getting divorces,

Spouses having affairs,

Young people living together,

And, babies having babies,

All at the same rate as the "non-churched" in America.

I knew that wasn't right. And I even could identify the problem.

Just before Jesus left the earth, he told his followers to "make disciples." He had just spent three years with his disciples so I have to believe that they had a pretty good idea what he meant when he said "make disciples."

He wanted them to share their lives with others and teach them the principles of the kingdom just like he had taught them the principles of the kingdom. They had had many, many conversations. They had spent time together. They had had the opportunity to watch Jesus live his life from week to week.

So, Jesus goes back to heaven. The Day of Pentecost hits. Three thousand become followers of Jesus Christ. Things kick into high gear. The disciples are preaching. People are joining every day. The new church is pooling its resources so that everyone has provisions.

In short, everyone starts to get really busy with the "work of the Lord."

Not that there's anything wrong with being busy with the work of the Lord. But Jesus didn't say that we should be busy with the work of the Lord. He said we should "make disciples."

When I look at the organized church in America, I see people going to church, I see them paying their tithes, I see them sitting in Sunday School classes. I see them sitting in a pew during a service. I see them attending small groups. I see them supporting missionaries. I see them doing a lot of stuff.

If all that "stuff" resulted in mature disciples, we would see a church renowned for its love, mercy and servanthood.

Instead we see:

Couples getting divorced,

Spouses having affairs,

Young people living together,

And, babies having babies.

At the same rate as the "non-churched" in America.

To me, it was obvious that we were not making disciples, we were recruiting club members.

There was a glimmer of hope though.

For years, I had taken my daughter to breakfast on Saturdays. It gave us a chance to talk. And then I started taking my future son-in-law out to dinner every week so I could get to know him better and share my life with him.

Then one day, I decided to start the "un-church." It wasn't the "anti-church" because I still think church is a wonderful thing. A body of believers can do things that no individual can do on his or her own.

But I was tired of doing nothing to make a substantial difference the lives of others.

So...I took advantage of the opportunities that came my way.

When a young man received discouraging news regarding the health of his fiancé, I took him to breakfast. And then I took him to breakfast again. And then I took him to breakfast again. And when he and his fiancé married, we continued going to breakfast.

When another young man wanted to know more about music, I took him to dinner and kept taking him to dinner.

When a young husband opened up one Sunday and told me that he didn't have anyone to talk to, I took him to dinner as well and kept taking him to dinner.

When a young father admitted that his life with Christ wasn't all he wanted it to be, I took him to dinner as well.

As of the time of this writing, I am *still* taking them to dinner, every week that our schedules permit.

We talk. We share our lives. We learn from each other.

The process isn't instantaneous. It takes time. But we are all getting stronger.

And someday, I hope that each of them will find others with whom to share their lives.

It's so very simple.

Who is helping you to be a more mature disciple of Jesus Christ? Whom are you helping become a more mature disciple of Jesus Christ?

As long as you're alive, it should be one or the other. Even better, it should be both.

how CERTAIN *our ignorance*

As already mentioned, I wrote a book called *The Nitpicker's Guide for X-philes*, in the 1990s. For those of you who don't know, *The X-Files* was a popular television show featuring FBI agents investigating the paranormal. The last screen of the opening credits normally featured some type of terse tag line. The most popular was "The Truth Is Out There."

While this idea of searching for the truth was the underlying theme of *The X-Files*, the writers of *The X-Files* aspired to more than the simple chase and a tidy ending. The writers engaged in a deeper exploration that ventured into a branch of philosophy called epistemology.

Epistemology is the study of questions like "How do we know what we think we know?" and "How do we decide that we know something?"

The X-Files presents two archetypes for "knowing," represented by its two FBI agents.

Fox Mulder is a subjectivist. Given the slightest connection between pieces of evidence, he jumps to a conclusion and is completely convinced that reality is exactly as he believes. In short, Mulder establishes truth simply because he believes that a certain thing is true.

Dana Sculley is an objectivist. She demands conclusions verified by rigorous, repeatable experiments. When she says that the truth is "out there," she means that the truth exists whether she believes it or not and its very existence is a call to discovery through careful investigation.

What fascinated me most about *The X-Files* was that the creators of the series wrote scenes where Mulder and Sculley sabotage their quest for the truth. The creators of this series understood that the *true* quest of the characters was the validation of their decisions about how they derive their beliefs...not the truth itself (i.e. the characters want to be "right" more than they want to be "true.")

At one point, the creators even have Mulder say that if he dies it will be with the certainty that his "faith has been righteous." And while Scully—during a particular scene—acknowledges that several aspects of the current case suggest paranormal phenomena she adds that she is convinced that to accept a paranormal conclusion would be to "abandon all hope of understanding the scientific events behind them."

In other words, Mulder is comfortable with the truth so long as it validates his intuition and Scully is comfortable with the truth so long as it can be verified by her science.

This is an amazingly accurate analysis of human behavior. The creators are absolutely correct that humans spend a great deal of time defending their core assumptions.

What grows out of the defense is a "certain ignorance" — an expectation that the world is supposed to be exactly as we assume it to be, all the while "ignoring with certainty" other possibilities.

Two examples from the real world, one scientific, the other entertaining:

First, stem cell research.

Several years ago, there was a parade of scientists telling us that it was imperative for us to have unrestricted government-sponsored funding of research using embryonic stem cells. The overall impression communicated by this campaign was that stem cells were a rare commodity that could only be obtained by extracting them from embryos and the benefits of utilizing these stem cells held such promise that we should all just set aside any ethical concerns that we might have over treating human life like a crop to be harvested.

Much to the shock and disgust of these scientists, the President of the United States allowed the research but only with lines of stem cells that were already established.

Given that we are several years down the road from that parade, it might be interesting to look back and see what has transpired.

We now know that there are many sources for stem cells, all with their own unique characteristics and none of the additional sources have the same ethical concerns as embryonic stem cells.

There are many therapies available and approved using "adult" stem cell research.

But as of this writing, I cannot find any verified therapies that are in use from embryonic stem cells. All I find is phrases like "resultant treatments could have significant medical potential."

More interesting, it appears to be possible to produce stem cells from almost any other human cell through a bit of genetic manipulation.

And even more interesting, embryonic stem cell lines have been generated without the destruction of the source embryos.

To summarize, all the potential healing that we were given as a justification for the destruction of human life has yet to materialize and advances in science now mean that the destruction wasn't required in the first place.

But at the time of the debate there was a "certain ignorance" surrounding these possibilities.

Why?

Because those pushing the debate wanted more to be "right" than to find the cures that they trumpeted.

They wanted the rest of us to affirm that human life should be treated as a commodity. They wanted us to ally ourselves with their belief that we are all just biological machines.

The second example comes from the entertainment industry.

In 2008, Electronic Arts released a game called Spore. All the early press about Spore indicated that it was a game that traced the process of evolution from a single-celled organism through galactic empires.

Except, the first time I saw a short demo of the game, the mechanism for developing the characters consisted of the game player selecting different options for his or her character.

While it is technically correct to call this process "evolving," the term "evolution" has a heavy connotation in our society of a "random, undefined process."

In other words, in order to have a game which supposedly followed the process of evolution, it was necessary for the game creators to put the player in the role of a Master Architect...which places the game squarely in the realm of Intelligent Design. (And, yes, I realize that playing a game that follows a completely random, undefined process would be no fun at all because...what's the point of staring at a computer screen for three billion years?)

Yet, despite the game emulating intelligent design more than a random, undefined processes, the vast majority of early game reviews chose the word "evolve" to describe the game play instead of words like "design" or "plan."

Why?

Because the intelligent design aspect of the game was ignored with certainty.

This is the activity of the flesh.

And if you find yourself at this moment shaking your figurative fist at the individuals described above, I would hasten to add that your fist shaking is also an activity of the flesh.

My point in giving you these examples is not for you to judge those individuals. My point is to help you recognize a pattern in their behavior and then use that pattern to determine if you are engaged in the same behavior.

The basic principle is that the flesh will push you to ignore with certainty any avenue of thought that will disrupt the worldview that it is has crafted within you.

If you hear yourself barking things like "Well, that won't work"; "Oh, no, I could never do that"; or the famous "We've never done it that way before," take a moment to listen and consider if you are ignoring with certainty important avenues of investigation.

You might find solutions where you least expect them.

male AND female

(Fill in the blank below with "man" or "woman" depending on your sex.)

Pretend we are enjoying a meal together. At one point, I look up and ask:

"When you say, 'I'm a ____', what does that mean?"

Many times, when I ask this question, I get blank stares and halting answers that have nothing to do with truth. Eventually, the question gets tossed back to me and I answer.

"When I say, 'I'm a man,' it means that I have an X chromosome and a Y chromosome. If you're a woman, it means that you have two X chromosomes. And anyone who tries to tell you anything different is selling something."

For instance, if someone tries to tell you that shiny, healthy-looking hair will make you more of a woman, it's probably because that person wants to sell you some kind of hair product.

Think about all the ways advertisers push products at us.

If you drink the right beer, you'll be more of a man because you'll be able to attract better looking women.

If you dress more flagrantly, you'll be more of a woman because you'll be able to turn the heads of more men.

I could fill this entire book with specific marketing examples but the bottom line in most marketing campaigns is this:

"You are deficient as a human being in general and as an example of your sex in specific and you need products to help you be...*more.*"

By now, I'm hoping that you can see that this is just another tactic by the flesh within you and the conglomeration of flesh outside you to create noise in your existence.

But, as always, it's more than just an effort to create noise. It's also an effort to distract us from the truth — to distract us from the profound answer to the following question:

Why did God make male and female?

God didn't need to settle on two sexes for the procreation of the species. In nature, we have examples of life that buds asexually (i.e. without two sexes). God is a good designer. He could have designed us as a "household of three" (a *ménage a trios*) with one sex labeled "A" and another "B" and other "C". Or he could have constructed a foursome...or more.

Why two?

The answer is scattered throughout the entire Bible. There are multiple places in the Old Testament that refer to Israel as God's bride. There are multiple places in the New Testament that refer to believers as the Bride of Christ.

But the Apostle Paul gives us the clearest indications to reveal the mystery of bi-sexual construction.

In Philippians, Paul turns an interesting phrase in one of his prayers. In chapter 3, verse 10, he says, "I want to know Christ and the power of his resurrection and the fellowship of sharing in his sufferings, becoming like him in his death." (NIV)

I'm told that the word "know" is a Greek word that can be transliterated into the Hebrew word "know", as in the King James Version of Genesis when it says "And Adam knew Eve his wife; and she conceived, and bare Cain."

Paul is equating the deep intimate knowledge of conception with the kind of knowledge that he wishes to experience with the Divine.

And if that's not explicit enough for you, look at Ephesians 5:22-33. In these verses, Paul draws an absolute parallel between the relationship of a husband and wife and the relationship of Christ to the church—including sexual intercourse because Paul quotes from Genesis when he recalls the verse, "For this reason a man will leave his father and mother and be united to his wife, and the two will become one flesh." (NIV)

These things lead me to conclude that the reason God made male and female was to give us an inescapable illustration of the relationship that he wishes to have with us.

Certainly, the flesh within all of us is doing its best to corrupt this illustration. And I'll touch on some of those efforts in other chapters. But imagine for a moment, the most wonderful relationship that can be enjoyed between a man and a woman — the closeness, the joy, the intimacy and the love.

This is what God wants to have with you.

And he made male and female to give you a reminder of what your relationship with him can be.

That example is complete. No additional products are required. No matter what the marketers try to tell you.

sowing AND reaping

I find it sad that such a fundamentally important concept like "sowing and reaping" has been co-opted in our spiritual vocabulary. These days whenever a television ministry preaches "sowing and reaping," it's usually trying to convince you to send money (i.e. sow your "seed faith") so that God will bless you (i.e. you will "reap a harvest").

The concept of sowing and reaping is far more profound than this and it is a concept that every individual who lives in an agrarian setting instinctively understands.

The concept of sowing and reaping is simple: Everything grows.

Everything requires preparation; everything requires implantation and everything requires cultivation if it is to satisfy your expectations (i.e. if you expect to gain a harvest from it).

Unfortunately, many of us do not live in an agrarian society; we live in an information society. Information societies highlight results and hide process.

Want to watch television? Flip a switch. Want to watch a movie? Pick it from the shelf (or download it). Need a question answered? Get it from the Internet.

And you can do all these things…now.

In every case we have no first-hand experience of the processes that were required to create these products. In fact, in some cases, the products are specifically built to hide this effort (i.e. we are asked to "suspend our disbelief").

The result is an expectation that life is "all harvest."

But this expectation is false.

And, it will lead to failure.

Instead, make the most of your preparations when you undertake any new endeavor. Be careful to embrace experience before you embrace certainties (i.e. don't think you know how to do something before you've actually done it). Expect to make mistakes and expect to grow from them.

All of these things are part of the basic process of life.

For instance, in 2006, I got tired of not having high-speed internet at my house seven miles north of Springfield, Missouri. I'm a computer consultant and I have high-speed internet at my clients but I would come home to dial-up (and it was *slow* dial-up because the copper in my area is so old that it only supports 26 kbps).

However, while I know how to build applications—and while I have a neighbor who knows just about everything there is to know about computer hardware and networks—I didn't say, "Well...putting up a wireless internet service provider (WISP) business can't be that hard. I'll just buy some equipment and we'll figure it out as we go!"

Instead, I double-checked with all the major internet service providers in my area to confirm that none of them were heading my way.

I also found a guy who ran a WISP south of Springfield and paid him $150.00 for an hour of his time. We got together at a local restaurant. I brought my topographical maps and I asked him every question that I could think of and then ask him if there was anything that I didn't think to ask.

I also scoured the internet for the best reference book that I could find. I ordered it and read it cover to cover.

Before I purchased any equipment, I printed up yellow information sheets and hung them on almost every door within a one mile radius of my house. And when the phone calls didn't come pouring in, I went door-to-door, introducing myself to people, explaining what I was thinking about doing and asking if they would be interested in high-speed internet as well.

In other words, I did my preparations to the best of my ability.

But even with all my fastidious preparations I did not expect that I wouldn't make mistakes and that everything would proceed flawlessly because "there ain't no substitute for doin' it."

And I knew that once I started "doin' it," I would learn a great deal more. And...I did.

I could tell you many stories of how God has helped with this little side business. I could tell you many stories how it has allowed me to serve my neighbors.

The important point here is that I followed the pattern of sowing and reaping.

I began with careful preparation. I started small. I grew at a sustainable rate. I paused at strategic times to insure that everything was stable.

And now, I reap a harvest of about $500 in profits every month from it. Granted, that's not much but it means that this little business called "zarks.net" is on track to break even in December of 2009 (just slightly ahead of schedule).

And...I have high speed internet! (And, far more knowledge about setting up wireless links than I did two years ago.)

This is the first lesson to apply from the concept of sowing and reaping. It is the internal reason and it will help you in the projects that you undertake.

The second lesson to apply from the concept of sowing and reaping is external.

Don't insult others by assuming you know how easy it is for them to accomplish something in their field of expertise.

I always smile when I am conversing with a potential client and he or she says something like, "We need to do so and so and that shouldn't be that hard so how long will it take?"

Here's the problem: Everything seems easy from the outside because our flesh likes to diminish the concept of sowing and reaping (the concept of process). It does this so that we will underestimate the effort that is involved in any endeavor. That way it can later use that underestimation as a device to discourage and dishearten us later.

Instead of blundering into that trap, it is far better to phrase the question above in these terms: "We would like to do so and so, how should we proceed to gain a better understanding of the work effort that would be involved?"

Do you see the difference in the questions? The former question denies process and seeks to get results without recognizing any effort. The latter question respects process and seeks to enlist the knowledge of one who has been through the process at least once already.

And, if you will approach your business associates with the latter attitude you will find them much more likely to help you succeed.

health

There is no mystery to good health.

Most of us can achieve it by simply following these guidelines:

Don't smoke.

Exercise.

Eat a healthy diet.

Maintain a healthy weight.

Drink enough water.

Don't cheat on your sleep.

I doubt anyone reading that list was surprised by anything on it.

We all know what we should be doing with our bodies.

We all know how to create an environment of success in our bodies.

Yet, too many of us allow our flesh to drive us into making choices that create an environment of failure and then we're shocked when we have some kind of major medical event.

I turned fifty this year (2008), but when most people meet me they assume that I'm in my early forties and some think I'm in my thirties. I will admit that I have inherited a good set of genes. But for *years* I have also attempted to exploit the wonderful nutritional advantages that we enjoy in the United States of America. I have attempted to exercise, to drink plenty of water and to get adequate rest.

What possible reason could there be for a person to do otherwise, to knowingly drive his or her physical body into a state of disrepair?

There is every reason in the world if the "driver" hates the person involved.

The only question is: Will you allow your flesh to continue to con you into destroying yourself or will you embark on a program to tune up your body (if you need to do so)?

Remember that there's more at stake here than just living to be 100. Medical studies have shown that abdominal fat produces hormones and proteins that affect the body, cause inflammation and may be instigators of many diseases like dementia, cancer, heart disease and diabetes.

That sounds like "noise" to me.

The more noise in your system, the harder it will be to hear the voice of the Eternal.

Is your cheeseburger worth that?

The easiest and simplest way to get a quick read on the state of your body is your "body mass index" (BMI) and your waist size. You can find BMI calculators all over the Internet. Just put in your height and weight and you'll get a number. Normal weight is 18.5 through 24.9. However, if you're a woman your waist should be 32.5 inches or less and if you're a man, your waist should be 35 inches or less.

You can whine and grunt and complain about this but the truth remains the same. Your life will be substantially improved when you lose the weight.

So why not start now?

the FIELD

One day, during meditation, I began to imagine my life as a field. In my mind I could see thoughts, words, actions and emotions floating toward me from all directions. Underneath each was the tiny seed of a belief.

Those beliefs were easy to miss. The thoughts were adventurous; the words, large; the actions compelling and the emotions, exciting.

It would have felt so natural to embrace them all.

But, I could see those tiny seeds of belief underneath and I knew that once I embraced that thought or word or action or emotion, the belief would drop onto my field. Left to itself, it would start to grow. In time, it would produce its own seeds.

I realized, again, that I needed to guard my field.

I realized, again, that I needed to insure that the thoughts I entertained, the words I spoke, the actions I performed and the emotions I allowed held beliefs that would benefit my field.

I realized again that everything grows and the longer it grows, the more established it becomes.

If you allow yourself frustration, frustration will become the easier response to each successive challenge. But, if you purposefully embrace calm, calm will deepen and prepare you for the next task.

As I shared this with my family, my wife added an important observation:

It's far easier to pluck sprouts from the ground than it is to pull out a sapling. There are things that—once established—are very difficult to purge.

What have you been planting in your field?

Are there things that you once controlled that have grown to control you?

Is it time to pull certain attitudes up by the roots?

Whatever needs to be done: Do it quickly. Once the trunk begins to thicken, it will be much harder.

If you delay too long it will require a chainsaw and stump grinder.

And all of it grows out of those tiny seeds.

do FEEL *jellyfish* the OCEAN?

Next time you're outside, imagine a one inch square on the ground. Now imagine a square tube that grows straight into the sky, all the way into the vacuum of space.

Of course there is air inside that tube even though you can't see it and that air actually has some weight. In fact, if you are standing at sea level, the air in that square tube weighs approximately 14.7 pounds.

The truth is that we live at the bottom of an "ocean" of air. So the weight of the air around us isn't just pushing down on us from above, it is pushing against you from all sides, at somewhere around 14 pounds of pressure *per square inch.*

That's a lot of pressure.

Most of time we don't even feel it because we live with it every day. But occasionally, we drive into the mountains or we hop a ride on an airplane and we feel the pressure change.

There is an interesting meditative phase that some Christian mystics ponder when thinking about God:

"Boundless ocean, who can sound thee?"

I love that. I love thinking about God like that.

For those of you who might not be familiar with the verb "sound", it means to try to measure the depth of a body of water by letting down a rope with a weight.

The phrase is describing God as a great boundless expanse, an expanse that is beyond any attempt to measure its depth.

I have only added one perspective to this phrase as I have meditated on it. I do not imagine myself bobbing on the divine ocean.

With the Divine, there is no single direction like below. He is all.

Just like the ocean of air that surrounds us, there has never been a moment when God has not surrounded us. The Psalmist David performs a thought experiment on this when he asks in Psalm 139 if he could ever escape from God's presence. And, of course, he concludes that there is nowhere he can go to remove himself from the presence of the Divine.

Right now, God completely surrounds you. He completely infuses you. If you aren't aware of him, it's because you have grown used to all that he does for you.

You've grown used to his provision.

You've grown used to his kindness.

You've grown used to his love.

Do jellyfish feel the ocean?

Probably not.

But they should.

shame

Shame is the stick that the flesh beats you with after it throws away the carrot.

This tactic is particularly insidious.

The flesh continually says, "He's hot," to the young woman. It has her imagine his embrace. It tells her that he will truly love her, even though she knows he has a reputation for discarding his lovers. It makes her perspire. It makes her flutter.

Caught up in the cacophony of her flesh, she spends the night with him.

She wakes to find him gone.

He won't return her call.

He sneers when she attempts to meet him in person.

Now, the flesh employs different tactics.

"How dare he treat you that way!" it exclaims, when it knew full well that he would. That's why it picked the young man to be the "enthraller."

It also imitates the young man's sneer and hisses, "You slut."

It flogs her with every belief that it can, hoping to produce the destructive emotions that it desires:

"All men are liars."

"No one will ever love you."

"If you weren't so hideous looking, he would have stayed."

And when it finds one that resonates with the young woman, it pounds her harder.

If she has any religious inclinations, the flesh even attempts to pawn itself off as the voice of God (although if she truly understood God's love for her she would realize that God never condemns). Or, it imitates the voice of her parents.

Anything to drive her into isolation.

And just as she is about to resign herself to her loneliness, it feeds her enough hope to convince her to try again.

Not surprisingly, it picks another young man with the same characteristics as the first.

The cycle starts again.

Each time, her flesh uses the shame stick to pound its lies deeper into her heart. The more she embraces them, the faster she is bound by them.

If any of this sounds familiar, you already know that these cycles do not create an environment of success.

But you can, at any point in the cycle turn yourself towards a better path.

If you find yourself enthralled, you should pause and review the reasons for your attraction. Ask yourself: Does this person really have the qualities that it takes to build a life together?

If you find yourself forsaken, admit that you allowed yourself to be deceived. Admit that your circumstances are your own doing and resolve to be wiser.

If you are hopeless, find your quest. Build a satisfying life by embracing your epic.

Earn a quality partner by being a quality partner.

Allowing yourself to be beaten by the shame stick won't earn you any experience points that you can use later in life because the stick is filled with lies.

God doesn't need your penance.

He derives no pleasure from your flagellations.

He simply desires your embrace.

with the playing BOX

It's an often-heard moment.

The young child receives a large present. Eventually, the tiny hands rip away the wrapping paper. At some point, parents usually help. They're tired of waiting to see the delight on their child's face. Excitement erupts as all is revealed.

Moments later, the toy lays discarded and the young child spends the rest of the evening playing with the box. Parents smile with reservation. Some even wonder out loud if they should have saved themselves the effort and expense and simply purchased the box.

The Eternal has given each of us a box filled with hidden treasure. Of course, the boxes themselves aren't too shabby. Most of us enjoy five marvelous senses that allow us to experience the world. We have an incredible muscular and skeletal system that affords us great flexibility and mobility. Our brains are capable of analyzing and categorizing multiple simultaneous inputs.

In short—as the Psalmist David observed—we are "fearfully and wonderfully made." We have everything we need to interface with this world and express the unique wonders that lie within us.

But too often, we end up playing with the box instead exploring the frontiers of our capabilities.

We become so enamored with certain tastes and smells that we eat ourselves into obesity.

We gorge ourselves so thoroughly on entertainment—on sights and sounds—that our muscles atrophy from lack of use.

We become so preoccupied with pleasure—with touch— that our craving for it fills every waking moment and even drives us to illicit drugs and alcohol.

Our lives devolve into a drone for the next sensual experience while the greatness that we were born to express sits discarded in the corner.

If you doubt that your life has become addicted to smells and tastes, I offer you a simple test:

For one week, eat as much as you like as often as you like...

But only fresh fruits, fresh vegetable and raw nuts.

Don't eat anything that's cooked. Don't eat anything that comes in a box, bottle or can. No seasonings, no sugar, no salt. Don't eat anything that is processed. No coffee, no tea, no soda.

Drink water. (Okay, you can have bottled water because that's so convenient.)

I'm amazed at the responses that I get when I suggest this.

"I don't really eat a lot of fruit."

"I don't like vegetables."

"No meat?!"

"What's the point of living if you have to eat like that?"

"You're trying to take all the joy out of life!"

As someone who grew up in a country where people lived in the landfill and fought for the best position when the garbage truck dumped their loads just because they were hoping to find something edible, I find these reactions driven by the flesh.

God has provided wonderful nutritious food for us and we turn up our noses at it. We're like the spoiled child who sits at the dinner table and sneers, "I don't really like that and I don't have to eat it if I don't want to."

And then we trot off to feed at establishments that have spent millions of dollars to refine the taste of their food simply to entice us to return again and again.

Honestly, do you really believe that these establishments care what their meals are doing to your body? Of course not, they are a collective institution of humans that is driven by a conglomeration of flesh that not only wants to separate you from your money but spread as much destruction as it can...all the while convincing you that their food tastes "yummy."

The same can be said for the packaged food that comes from the grocery store. The primary concerns of the companies that create packaged foods are shelf-life, profit and how to make their products sire hunger so that you'll eat more of them. Your health and your success are way down on their list.

As a further consideration, rehearse the story of Daniel, Hananiah, Mishael and Azariah (aka Shadrach, Meshach Abednego). In the book of Daniel, chapter one, we learn that these four men are captured and taken to Babylon. When they arrive, they are put into a training regimen to serve in the king's palace.

They are to be fed from the king's table but Daniel immediately recognizes that the royal food and wine are not kosher and he asks the palace official for permission to eat only vegetables and drink only water for ten days. When the trial concludes, the palace official observes that the four young men look healthier and better nourished then the ones who indulged themselves.

It's easy for us to conclude that God supernaturally propped them up because they honored his word.

But I think there's a simpler principle at work in the story: God designed your senses and they are delightful but if you allow yourself to be lead by them you will create cravings that will generate noise and make it more difficult for you to hear the whispers of the Divine.

That's why I'm not surprised by the postscript to the story in Daniel: "In every matter of wisdom and understanding about which the king questioned [Daniel, Hananiah, Mishael and Azariah], he found them ten times better than all the magicians and enchanters in his whole kingdom." (Daniel 1:20 NIV)

Obviously, I've focused just on taste and smell in the last few paragraphs but the principle is the same for every sensation. God made them. He expects us to enjoy them but if they become our focus, they will distract us from the treasure that is within us.

Instead of gorging on your senses, take advantage of the wonderful opportunities that are available to you:

Learn a language.

Take up painting.

Write a novel.

Study history.

Enroll in classes at your local college or university.

Develop new skills.

Stretch yourself.

It doesn't matter if you're the best in the world at whatever you choose, your life will become richer simply through the effort.

Or…you can just sit on the couch, eat popcorn and watch movies all day but I don't recommend the latter if you want to create an environment of success for yourself.

(And in case you are wondering, no, I am not a vegan. If I am offered food that I wouldn't normally choose for myself, I consume it with gladness and thanks because God is a great designer and I am capable of processing other forms of nutrition. But…there's no question in my mind that my body is designed for — and functions best with — the foods that this world produces on its own.)

RACE relations

I am always amused when someone is branded a "racist."

The simple truth is this: The flesh in all of us is racist. And it's sexist. And it's whatever other divisive term you want to assign to it.

The flesh in each of us hates us and it hates every other being around us so why *wouldn't* it be racist?!

As I have mentioned and will mention several times in this book, one of the classic strategies of the flesh is to cause you to focus outward to keep you distracted from focusing inward. And certainly, the color of a person's skin is one of the easiest ways to categorize humans. So, of course, the flesh is going to attempt to use that to carve humanity into separate camps and convince you that the only place you are safe is with "your own kind."

The sooner we recognize that we are all racist and that there's a part of us that will always be racist, the sooner we can start acting in ways that reduce the expression of that racism.

For instance, I try to keep my head up while grocery shopping and greet people. I *especially* do this with people who are a different race than I.

What do you think happens when I greeting individuals with "Good morning, sir (or ma'am). How are you today?"? Most of the time, the person smiles and returns the greeting. This little exercise, performed consistently, does much to dampen the grumblings from my flesh that this or that person should be feared/avoided/condemned/ignored because of the color of his or her skin.

But as long as we're willing to accept the foolishness that this person is racist and that person isn't...

As long as we're willing to listen to the flesh within us telling us that there is "us" and "them"...

Racism will continue to manifest in the world.

I'm trying to do my part on a daily basis to change this.

How about you?

CAGE fighting

Your flesh has spent your entire lifetime building a cage around you. It does it with "bars" that sound like this:

"I'm not good at ____."

"That's just not my gifting."

"Oh, I could never do ____."

"I'm just hot tempered."

"Well, my father/mother was like that too."

It builds this cage so that it can convince you to quit trying to accomplish the things that you're capable of accomplishing.

And, if you dare even think about trying to accomplish something outside the cage? It crawls inside the cage and starts slamming you against the bars to remind you that they exist.

And, if somehow you manage to walk out the open door that your flesh can never fully seal? It will brow-beat you with a vengeance the first time you trip and stumble back in.

Wonderfully enough, the only thing that keeps you inside the cage is...you.

And the door is open.

when the TOWER fell

One day, several months ago, while driving south on National Avenue in Springfield, Missouri, I came to a stop at the intersection of National and Chestnut Expressway. The city was widening the intersection and it had installed temporary traffic lights strung between wooden telephone poles.

On the far side of the intersection I saw a sports utility vehicle waiting to turn south onto National from Chestnut. In what seemed like slow motion, I saw one of the telephone poles begin to tilt. A moment later it fell, bouncing off the hood of the SUV before coming to rest on the ground in front of the vehicle. Of course it pulled all the traffic lights to the ground with it and they clattered for another moment before everything settled to silence.

I thought to myself, "Now, there's something you don't see every day."

The man in the SUV got out and gave the pole a confused stare. He seemed fine and his car didn't appear to be damaged too severely so I snapped a couple of photographs and detoured down Chestnut Expressway.

I can imagine his reaction.

"Are you *kidding* me? What did I do to deserve this?!"

At least, that would be his reaction if he's like most of us.

So, what is the belief beneath this reaction?

"I deserve to live each day the way I want to live it without anything interrupting me and certainly without anything that gets in the way of me doing what I want to do. No bad things! Just happy times."

Jesus had some interesting comments about this in Luke chapter 13. At the beginning of the chapter, some in his audience tell Jesus that Pilate has killed a group of Galileans. Apparently, this group of Galileans were offering a sacrifice of some kind — perhaps at the temple in Jerusalem — and Pilate sent in his men to kill them while they were making their sacrifice.

The motive of those telling this story is unclear: Maybe they wanted Jesus to speak out against Pilate; maybe they were insinuating that these Galileans had done something to deserve their fate; maybe they were looking for a bit of empathy or assurance.

Instead of doing any of those things, he asks two pointed questions:

"Do you think these Galileans were worse sinners than all the other Galileans because they suffered this way? I tell you, no! But unless you repent, you too will all perish. Or those eighteen who died when the tower of Siloam fell on them—do you think they were more guilty than all the others living in Jerusalem? I tell you, no! But unless you repent, you too will perish." (Luke 13:2-5 NIV)

Before talking about Jesus' proposed solution, let's focus on his observation about life in general. In essence, Jesus is saying this: Don't make excuses trying to explain away why bad things happen to people in an effort to make yourself feel more secure. Don't vilify others. Don't think they must have some secret sin that condemned them to their fate.

Rather, understand the truth: Life is dangerous. It doesn't come with a child-proof cap. There may be times when you are driving along, minding your own business and a telephone pole will fall on you!

Put simply, don't question why bad things happen to others. Instead, remind yourself that the same tragedy could just as easily overtake you.

This attitude will do a number of things for you. It will make you more compassionate. It will give you more realistic expectations. It will make you more grateful for every day that disaster doesn't strike.

And it should motivate you to keep an open communication with the Divine, to change your mind for the better...which is what Jesus means when he says, "repent."

(Of course, if you decide to repent, your flesh will immediately go into bargaining mode and try to tell you that if you follow Jesus' instruction to the letter then you won't have any problems in life. The flesh does this—not because it believes it to be true—but because it is trying to trick you into false expectations so that it can pound you with doubts the next time a problem comes your way. Remember…it's sneaky.)

On the other hand—to bring balance to this discussion—I should add there is certainly more than one kind of danger in the world. And the dangers that we encounter *can* be the result of our own actions. But, that's a topic for another chapter.

SAND castles

One day as I was reading Jesus' Sermon on the Mount (Matthew 5-7) I came to the parable of the wise and foolish builders. Most likely, you are familiar with the parable:

The wise man built his house on the rock. The storms came and the house stood.

The foolish man built his house on the sand. The storms came and the house crumbled.

The standard interpretation of the parable is that when a person accepts Jesus Christ as his or her savior, that person has built his or her house on the "rock."

Except…if you read the Sermon on the Mount, you'll see that Jesus tells us what the parable means and the standard interpretation is not the interpretation that Jesus gives.

Listen to the entire parable from Matthew 7:24-27 (NIV), "Therefore everyone who hears these words of mine and puts them into practice is like a wise man who built his house on the rock. The rain came down, the streams rose, and the winds blew and beat against that house; yet it did not fall, because it had its foundation on the rock. But everyone who hears these words of mine and does not put them into practice is like a foolish man who built his house on sand. The rain came down, the streams rose, and the winds blew and beat against that house, and it fell with a great crash."

There is only one interpretation for this parable: Jesus said that if you hear "these words of mine" and *put them into practice,* your life will be built on a rock. If you just hear the words of Jesus and don't put them into practice, you're a fool and when the storms come, you will be in deep trouble.

Very few times has anyone raced past me to the punch-line in this discussion. The rest of time, when I share this over dinner, the friend who sits across the table from me gets a startled look on his or her face because he or she has never heard this before.

But it gets better.

Since Jesus tells us that we need to hear and do "these words of mine" it would be a really good idea if we knew what words he is talking about.

The parable comes at the end of the Sermon on the Mount. It is Jesus' concluding statement. He is obviously referring to his just-preached sermon.

So, then the question becomes: What did Jesus say in the Sermon on the Mount?

The sad truth is that there are very few of us who can recall, off-hand, what Jesus said in those three chapters of Mathew.

Let's recap.

If we believe Jesus Christ is our personal savior, we probably also believe that our lives are built on a rock.

Except...

We aren't really sure what Jesus said in the Sermon on the Mount.

And, if we can't remember what he said, there's a good chance we aren't putting his words into practice.

And, if we aren't putting them into practice, Jesus said that our lives are built on sand.

Since entire books have been written on Matthew five, six and seven, I'm only going to pull out one example. (Hopefully, you will find the time in the next few days to read the Sermon on the Mount verse by verse and make notes.)

In Matthew 6:25, Jesus tells us not to worry about our lives.

He doesn't say, "Try to reduce your worrying by ten percent each week."

He says, "Stop worrying. Don't do it."

The question is: Do you worry? Because if you worry, you are not putting Jesus' words into practice and you are building your house on sand.

That may seem like a harsh statement until you realize that the core belief of worry is that God is either unwilling or unable to care for us. By worrying, you cultivate that belief in your heart and that belief will increase the noise in your life and drown out the voice of the Divine.

It's not that God will punish you if you worry, it's that worry will—on its own—create an environment of failure around you. That's why Jesus doesn't want you to worry. And in a larger sense, that's why Jesus wants you to hear his words and put them into practice.

VS. ISOLATION *community*

As I've mentioned elsewhere, when I'm out and about I try to keep my head up and greet people.

"Good morning! How are you today?"

Occasionally, I get a cold stare but for the most part, people smile and greet me back.

I have a little saying to characterize this activity.

"Community is better than isolation."

One day as I was grocery shopping, I passed a person and only later realized I had intentionally ignored the person. I replayed the moment and realized my flesh had shuddered and quite forcefully commanded, "Don't talk to her!"

What was this woman's great crime that condemned her to be ignored instead of greeted with a kind word?

She was young and pretty. (And by "pretty," I mean extremely attractive.)

As I reviewed the reasoning behind my flesh's efforts in this matter, I found it lacking.

"So, just because a human happens to be female and happens to fall in the exact range of facial characteristics and body type that society deems the most desirable—at this point in the long continuum of characteristics and body types that society has rendered the same judgment on in times past—I'm supposed to shun her?!"

"Well," my flesh shot back, "She probably gets heckled by men all the time and she'll just think you're making a pass at her."

That didn't sound right to me so I ignored it and I remembered my saying, "Community is better than isolation."

Of course, it was all theoretical at that moment because I had already passed her and I certainly wasn't going to run her down because that *would* be weird. I trundled on confident that I had this new-found revelation firmly in place in my spirit and when the "next time" came, I would do better.

Several minutes later, I arrived at the checkout lanes. All of the lanes—except one—were fairly long. The short one was populated by...the pretty girl. (Everyone else was intimidated by her as well.)

Of course, my flesh tried the same tactic a second time and I started to fall for it again.

And then I thought, "Okay. This is *dumb*. It's the shortest line. Take it."

So, I did. And the spirit started whispering, "You should really say hello."

I let my flesh beat me up for a few seconds before I finally had enough of it. I noticed she was buying a car seat so I leaned forward and asked her how old her child was.

She jumped. Because...I'm sure...the only people who ever talk to her in stores are guys hitting on her.

So, I smiled and asked again. When she told me, we struck up a conversation about children and family and had the nicest little chat.

And when she left, I said, "Have a nice day!"

She smiled pleasantly and exited the store.

Two humans, having an adult conversation about the joys of life.

Community.

Several months later, my wife and I went to Branson, Missouri for a weekend get-away. That Saturday morning, I went for a quick run/walk. As I approached a new condominium development on Highway 76—the main road through town—a woman in her late twenties or early thirties stepped onto the sidewalk fifty feet ahead of me. She appeared to be out for some morning exercise as well.

Now I have a problem. I'm taller than she is. My legs are longer. I'm going to catch up to her in mere minutes and I'm approaching from behind, which is disconcerting.

"Community is better than isolation," I tell myself.

"Well yeah," the flesh says, "but you're just going to make her uncomfortable and for her sake you should really cross over to the other side of the street and leave her alone."

Sad to say, I listened and crossed over to the other side of the street.

Of course, ten minutes afterwards, I'm thinking, "That was dumb. You listened to your flesh. You knew it was your flesh and your flesh is always trying to create an environment of failure."

Then Sunday morning arrives. I get up; go out to get some exercise. I am not on the same schedule as the day before. I take a different route but at one point I pass the same condominium development. It's new and I'm always interested in buildings so I decide to take a short cut through the buildings. (There are several buildings in the complex.)

Randomly, I work my way through the development.

Then, off to my left I hear a door open. Moments later, twenty or so feet in front of me, I see a woman walk out between the cars. She turns left and appears to be heading for an SUV or mini-van. (I can't remember which.)

It's the same woman.

And the flesh starts sputtering the same line that it did the day before.

This time, however, I do muster up enough intestinal fortitude to smile and greet her.

But that's all I do. I don't do what I was supposed to do. And I know I didn't do it because I know what I should have done.

I should have said, "Good morning. My name is Phil Farrand. I am on a quest in my life to prefer community over isolation. To that end, I try to make a habit of greeting those that I encounter — to treat them with respect as a fellow human being and traveler through this life. However, while I was out for my morning exercise yesterday I actually saw you out for a walk and I crossed the street and purposefully ignored you. This morning I started at a different time and took a completely different route but I have encountered you again so I am taking this opportunity to apologize for my behavior yesterday. And, I hope you have a wonderful day."

Yes, dear reader, I know you think I'm crazy. But I also know that there is a depth of living that we are missing because we have allowed our flesh to bully us into isolation over community.

One final story, not because I need to rehearse my exploits with young women but because I really do have a reason for relating these events.

Several months later, I walked into Blockbusters with my wife. As is our habit, she took off in one direction looking for a movie that she would enjoy and I took off in another looking for a movie I would enjoy. As I worked my way around the edge of the store, I noticed…out of the corner of my eye…

Blonde hair, short shorts.

I'm a guy. I notice these things.

The young woman wearing the blonde hair and short shorts is standing in front of a bank of movies searching for something to watch.

I keep working my way toward her and eventually our paths cross. She's still staring intently at the movie. I take that as an excuse to say nothing.

Then she reaches down for *Sweeny Todd, the Demon Barber of Fleet Street*.

(For those of you who do not know, *Sweeny Todd*, the 2007 movie by Tim Burton stars Johnny Depp and is based on the 1979 hit Broadway musical by Stephen Sondheim which is based on the 1973 play by Christopher Bond. It is not a movie I recommend but the music is incredible.)

As I see her pick up *Sweeny Todd*, a whisper within me says, "Tell her the music in that movie is fabulous."

I promptly ignore the whisper even though I'm fairly certain it is from the spirit and not the flesh. I take a few more steps and the whisper gets louder and more forceful.

"Tell her the music in that movie is fabulous."

At this point, I know it's the spirit, so I spin and say, "Ya know, I can't really recommend that movie because there's a lot of gore in it but the music is *fabulous*."

She looked up and replied, "It is? I've looked at it a couple of times but I just wasn't sure." Then she looks at me again and says, "You do the music at Praise Assembly, right?" (For fifteen months, I was the interim music minister at Praise Assembly here in Springfield, Missouri.)

And we strike up a conversation. Moments later my wife joins us, we wander down the new releases and compare notes on those movies and then my wife and I go home.

We have a very nice conversation. Two human, talking about the movies they enjoy.

Community.

Turns out, the last time my wife and I had any contact with the young lady she was twelve but my wife remembered her as soon as they started visiting. (Me? I had no clue.)

I tell you these stories to illustrate that "knowing" is not "doing." I have known that community is better than isolation for years. But I am still learning to "be" community in all my interactions with fellow human beings.

and the **chicken little** LOTTERY

It's useful to remember that noisy, frantic emotions are always from the flesh.

For instance, if the stock market is plunging...

And you feel the panic rising within you...

And you hear, "Sell, sell, sell! Get out while you can! It's the end of the world!"

Take a moment to identify the culprit.

Recognize that the flesh is running around inside you, banging its little drum, doing a Chicken Little impersonation of that old favorite, *The Sky Is Falling*.

Recognize as well that…it's lying.

While it may be true that the *stock market* is falling, the *sky* is not falling because the Eternal is still the Eternal and your life is still hidden in him.

You have no way of knowing what the Dow Jones Industrial Average will be a year from now. You may have to make a few sacrifices. You may have a few adventures that you might not have chosen. But if those adventures require the stripping away of your comfort and that stripping proves useful for quieting the atmosphere of your life, you may someday be grateful for the experience.

(Besides, financial experts will tell you that the "panic" is the worst time to sell. If you sell, you'll never have the possibility of recouping your losses. And that's precisely why your flesh is trying to push you to sell. Because your flesh is dedicated to your destruction and it will always try to encourage you to take the most damaging course of action.)

Likewise, you should suspect any emotion that promises an immediate, sudden flood of ease into your life.

When you drive by the Powerball lottery sign that's flashing this week's jackpot…

And the jackpot is $253,000,000.00…

And the panting springs up in you to buy a lottery ticket because 253 million would make all your dreams come true…

Recognize that it's just the flesh baiting you. It knows the odds. It knows that the lottery is a tax on the mathematically-impaired.

(A friend of mine once saw a young couple come out of a gas station convenience store with lottery tickets in hand. Before performing the ritual "scratch-off," the couple clutched them tightly and began chanting, "Please, oh please, oh please...." Then, they checked all the tickets. No winners. They left the station with great disappointment. I'm guessing they were back the next week, wasting more money.)

Many years ago, I heard an old fable from China. It went something like this:

In a small village, a man once captured and tamed a magnificent horse. It was so beautiful that people came from miles around to admire it.

"It's a blessing!" they would cry out when seeing the horse, "Surely the gods are pleased with you to allow you to find such a valuable creature."

The man would always reply, "Say not that it's a blessing. Say not that it's a curse. Say only that I have found a magnificent horse."

One day the horse broke free of the man's pasture and could not be found.

"It's a curse!" his fellow villagers cried. "You've lost your most valuable possession. Surely you have done something to anger the gods. It must be a curse."

But, as before, the man simply replied, "Say not that it's a blessing. Say not that it's a curse. Say only that my horse has broken free of my pasture and is gone."

A few days later, the magnificent horse returned to the man and led twenty five other wild horses into his pasture. By law, the man now owned all twenty-six.

When word of the occurrence spread, all those who came to see for themselves exclaimed, "It's a blessing! How blessed and favored by the gods are you!"

The man remained steadfast. "Say not that it's a blessing. Say not that it's a curse. Say only that my horse has returned with twenty-five other horses."

Shortly afterwards, the man's son attempted to ride one of the wild horses and was thrown to the ground. The fall broke his leg.

"It's a curse," the villagers cried. "You must have become prideful because you're rich with horses and the gods have cursed you."

The man simply sighed and repeated, "Say not that it's a blessing. Say not that it's a curse. Say only that my son has fallen and broken his leg."

A week later, the great king came through the village, drafting every young man to fight against his enemies to the north. Those who went with the king all died in battle.

But the man's son lived because of the broken leg.

Obviously, at each stage, neither the man nor the villagers knew what the future held. Yet at each stage, the villages ran to the extremes and found failure whereas the man held his center and found success.

consuming the CONSUMER

In June of 2008, the Journal of Consumer Research published a study by Bram Van den Bergh, Siegfried Dewitte, and Luk Warlop called, "Bikinis Instigate Generalized Impatience in Intertemporal Choice."

In the study men were exposed to sexy stimuli. They were shown pictures of beautiful women. They watched video clips of young bikini-clad women running through the woods and down a beach. They were given bras to fondle.

Testing directly after these events revealed that the men weren't simply aroused sexually, their entire "rewards" system shifted in focus to the present. They experienced a generalized craving for anything pleasant. In other words, they wanted it now, not later…now. They disregarded consequence and reached for anything to give them a quick hit.

A buddy of mine heard a pair of radio personalities discussing the study and the radio personalities found it very odd that looking at a woman in a bikini would make a man reach for a donut.

My friend thought it made perfect sense. He understood that both activities are linked to the flesh (lust and overeating).

Even the researchers in the study concluded that there is one common appetite system in the brain and stimulating it in any way spills over into anything that the individual desires.

I think my friend is right. It does sound just like the flesh.

The principle is simple: Feed a craving, and you will only crave more. And eventually, the craving will feed on you.

That's because responding to a craving makes the flesh grow stronger in our lives and when the flesh grows stronger it wants more. It knows that "more" creates an environment of failure.

In other words, being a consumer simply means that you will be consumed. As your desires grow, you will need a greater supply. To get that greater supply (be it food, sex, drugs or alcohol), other areas of your life will be sacrificed.

For instance, I've always appreciated David Duchovny as an actor. He's obviously intelligent and brings that additional level to his craft. Unfortunately, he has also chosen roles that consistently feature a sexually promiscuous lifestyle. These choices have been so consistent that it seemed obvious to me that he lived by the "do what makes you feel good" rule.

In August of 2008, the major news organizations reported that David Duchovny voluntarily entered rehab for sexual addiction.

"I have voluntarily entered a facility for the treatment of sex addiction," the official statement read. "I ask for respect and privacy for my wife and children as we deal with this situation as a family."

The consumer had become the consumed. (And yes, your flesh is probably telling you, "But think about how much fun he had before he went into rehab!")

Of course, Jesus knew how this works. That's why he said, "If anyone would come after me, he must deny himself and take up his cross and follow me." (Matthew 16:24 NIV)

That statement isn't just a call for us to focus on him as a priority in our lives. It is a prescription for success because the person who willingly releases his or her cravings will quiet the voice of the flesh within and quieting the voice of the flesh within will allow you to hear the whispers of the Eternal.

(Of course, the flesh never gives up easily so as soon as you make the commitment to do this, it will sit in the corner and pout, "No fair. When am I going to get what I want? Jesus never lets me have any fun. Always have to carry the cross." If you listen to that voice, denying your cravings won't do you any good because you'll simply trade one kind of noise for another.)

PAIN

I only have a vague recollection of it.

I can't recall exactly when I heard it.

I remember I was young, no older than my early teens.

But I still remember the gist of it because it shaped one of my fundamental attitudes toward life.

This isn't the exact quote because I can't find the quote— and I have searched for it on goggle.com and amazon.com and several "famous quotation" sites.

It says something similar to this:

"I walked a year with Pleasure and learned nothing. I walked an hour with Pain and learned enough for a lifetime."

I think this quote resonated with me because I have always wanted to be wise. Not just to have knowledge, but to be able to apply it in ways that keep me from acting like a fool.

When I heard this saying, something within told me it was true and if it was true, pain was a friend and not an enemy. Pain could help me achieve my goal. Ever since, I have greeted pain with solemnity instead of fear.

Now, obviously, there are many kinds of pain.

When I was in elementary school I had an odd experience with a particular kind of pain. I was in the back yard of our house in the Republic of the Philippines. I was holding a stick that had a point on one end. I remember looking at it, thinking it would probably hurt if I stuck myself in the eye with it. And then...I proceeded to find out!

Okay, I didn't jam the stick in my eye but I made contact.

And I was right, it did hurt. I'm still not sure why I did it. One moment I'm thinking about it. After the next moment, I was hollering, "Ow!"

This is what I call foolish pain.

Unfortunately, too many of us, too many times, have a pretty good idea what the consequences will be when we do something foolish and instead of stopping to think for a moment, we just go right ahead and do it.

Granted, I did learn something that day: Don't poke yourself in the eye with a stick.

But, I think I could have probably acquired that piece of knowledge without having to spend the next several minutes rubbing my eye.

On the other hand, there are times when we should consciously and methodically subject ourselves to pain but only when we have a specific goal.

This is wise pain.

Jesus put it this way. "If anyone would come after me, he must deny himself and take up his cross and follow me." (Mark 8:34 NIV)

This statement comes on the heels of a series of encounters between Jesus and the disciples. It starts in Mark 8:27 when Jesus asks his disciples, "Who do people say I am?"

The disciples reply that some think he is John the Baptist, some think Elijah, some think he is one of the prophets.

When Jesus asks, "Who do you say I am?" Peter answers, "You are the Christ."

It is important to note here that when Peter says "You are the Christ," he really means, "You're the guy who is going to overthrow the Romans and set up a new monarchy and be our king and champion and you're going make all our dreams come true."

Of course, Jesus knows this is Peter's definition of "Christ." Consequently, Jesus launches into a lecture that indicates in no uncertain terms that, as Christ, he is going to suffer and be rejected and killed.

This revelation doesn't sit well with Peter. It isn't what he expects from his leader. So, taking Jesus aside, Peter tries to set him straight.

Jesus responds with the famous quote, "Get behind me, Satan! You do not have in mind the things of God, but the things of men." (Mark 8:33 NIV)

And then Jesus turns to those around him and says—in essence—"If you're with me, you're going to do the same thing that I'm about to do. You're going to set aside what you want. And you're going to submit yourself to the amount of pain that's necessary for you to die to your selfishness."

In other words, wise pain is the pain that we embrace with the specific goal of lessening the influence of the flesh in our lives. (And even foolish pain and be turned into wise pain by recognizing your responsibility in the pain and working through the consequences.)

(There's a whole side discussion we could have at this point comparing the commitment that was required from early Christians versus the commitment that is still required in many places across this world versus the commitment that is required here in American. I'll leave that for another time. Here's a preview: While an excruciating death was a very real possibility for early Christians, often the greatest sacrifice that we face is turning off the television and going to bed early enough so that we'll have time to start the next day with prayer.)

One last observation about pain: It seems to be that each of us is born "owing pain." I don't know who we owe it to and I don't know why some seem to have a greater debt than others. But each of us, at some point or points in our lives will make payments on our debt.

Personally, I prefer to make my payments with wise pain and in small increments. From what I've seen, paying with foolish pain rarely satisfies the debt and often increases it.

Of course, there are those who love to take advantage of "pain delays;" who never want to be inconvenienced, who want to do whatever they what to do whenever they want to do it.

If you happen to be one of those people, my only hope is that your pain doesn't choose to collect all those little missed payments in one lump sum.

BASIC husbandry

One day, over dinner, after talking to a friend about the role of a husband he looked at me and said:

"You know, if more men knew that, they probably wouldn't get married."

He was joking but I understood the point he was making. As men, we tend to think of marriage as "finding someone who will take care of me: cook, clean, believe in me, laugh at my jokes."

And we tend to define the role of a husband in terms we find comfortable.

A husband provides for his family.

A husband protects his family.

A husband leads his family.

Priest of his home. King of his castle. Adored by his wife.

(Insert grunt here.)

Not that the above list is all bad. A husband should provide for, protect and lead his family. But Paul gives us an analogy that paints the role of the husband in a different light.

In Ephesians 5:22-33 (NIV), Paul discusses the roles of husbands and wives. I'm always amazed how quickly we quote the first two verses of this passage. We start off strong with:

"Wives, submit to your husbands as to the Lord. For the husband is the head of the wife as Christ is the head of the church..."

We usually mumble through the next few words and then pick back up with verse 24, "Now as the church submits to Christ, so also wives should submit to their husbands in everything."

And then, when there's trouble or disagreements, we begin a litany:

"My wife doesn't support me like she should."

"My wife doesn't submit to my leadership."

"My wife doesn't love me like the church is supposed to love Christ."

On and on it goes, a diatribe that lays the blame for any failings in our marriages squarely on our wives because they aren't fulfilling their responsibilities.

But are we fulfilling ours?

In the verses that follow the verses we love to quote, Paul says this:

"Husbands, love your wives, just as Christ loved the church and gave himself up for her to make her holy."

In other words, the role of a husband is to do everything that he can do to be a redeeming influence in the life of his wife. The husband is called to imitate Christ and to sacrificially serve her in any way that he can so that she can become *everything* that God intends for her to be.

Christ was beaten for his bride.

Christ was mocked and spat on for his bride.

Christ was crucified and died for his bride.

What have you done for yours?

My daughter and son-in-law understood these principles before they married and they wanted to base their marriage vows on them. So, we had my father read this passage from The Message and then we paraphrased it for their vows.

My son-in-law pledged the following to my daughter:

"I, Alan Beauchamp, take you Elizabeth, to be my lawfully wedded wife.

"I pledge to learn a life of love from Christ, to love you with extravagance, to be courteously reverent toward you, out of respect for Christ.

"I pledge to provide leadership in our home, in the way that Christ leads the church, not by domineering but by cherishing.

"I pledge to model my love for you after the love that Christ has shown the church, doing my best to bring out the best in you using my words and deeds to evoke your beauty, giving my life to make you radiant.

"This I will do, as Christ and His Holy Spirit enable me."

To this my daughter responded:

"I, Elizabeth Farrand, take you Alan, to be my lawfully wedded husband.

"I pledge to learn a life of love from Christ, to love you with extravagance, to be courteously reverent toward you, out of respect for Christ.

"I pledge to understand and support you in ways that show my support for Christ.

"I will submit to your leadership as the true Church submits to Christ.

"I will honor you, as the true Church honors Christ.

"This I will do, as Christ and His Holy Spirit enable me."

After the wedding, someone jokingly asked if I had written the vows because Alan's portion seemed more demanding. Certainly, the husband's role in a marriage *is* more demanding but I didn't make it that way, God did.

Beyond being demanding, however, the role of the husband has other implications for us as men. We are in a unique position in the model that Paul reveals in Ephesians 5.

We are husbands to our wives and simultaneously the beloved of Christ.

This dual responsibility renders all our complaints utterly futile because, if we are honest with ourselves, we must constantly put ourselves to the test...in both directions.

If you find yourself grousing over your wife's lack of spirituality or maturity, you should ask yourself if you have sacrificed everything that you could to help her become the woman that she can be.

If you find yourself disappointed that your wife isn't as devoted to you as you might like, you should ask yourself if your devotion to Christ matches the level that you desire from your wife.

In all likelihood, the harsh truth is this: Everything you find lacking in your marriage can be traced to your neglect of your wife and/or your neglect of Christ.

Thankfully, you can start again today. You can build a strong marriage and a peaceful home but it will require two separate efforts.

First, rekindle (or kindle for the first time) your passion for Christ.

Second, rekindle (or kindle for the first time) your devotion to your wife's success.

On your own, without any change in your wife, you can have a profound, positive influence on your marriage.

In time, if you draw closer to Christ and serve your wife without any expectation in return, something beautiful will grow.

One final reflection: Over the past several years, many have sought to champion the sanctity of marriage by seeking legislation to define marriage as the union between a man and a woman.

I find that definition lacking. Marriage is more than the union between a man and a woman.

As designed by God, marriage is a holy covenant between a man as a husband following the example of Christ and a woman as a wife following the example of Christ's beloved. Any less cheapens the sanctity of marriage.

Certainly, men who have affairs cheapen marriage as an institution. But so do men who abuse their wives either physically or emotionally;

As do men who bark orders;

As do men who condescend;

As do men who accuse;

As do men who murmur.

In short, if your behavior, in any way, falls below the standard that Christ has set for us by sacrificing everything for his Beloved, you are cheapening the sanctity of marriage.

And it is my opinion that we would accomplish far more by becoming better examples of the real meaning of marriage than by attempting to pass laws which degrade its definition.

archetypes

For many years, I have been fascinated with human emotion. We have a phrase that we use around the house when we're watching a movie on Friday night and the movie concludes with a heart-rending scene.

As we reach for the tissues, we say, "Wow, that really hit the moment."

Or, if the tissues stay in the box we might say, "Didn't quite hit the moment, did they?"

This idea of "hitting the moment" came to me while I was working on the *Nitpicker's Guides*. Actually, it came to me while I was working on my first novel...while I was working on the *Nitpicker's Guides*.

Each *Nitpicker's Guide* took approximately seven months to write and each would finance the entire year. That meant I had a five-month "summer vacation" to work on my fiction.

One morning during summer vacation, while revisiting a small section of a chapter that I had edited multiple times, I suddenly understood what it was missing.

I changed a few words, added a phrase or two, polished the tone of the section a bit and suddenly it "hit the moment." I started to cry. And others cried as well.

It was like I had found a lock on the human heart and if I crafted my words using just the right sequence I could turn the lock and open the reader's emotions.

It was the deep magic.

That day, I knew I could never be fully satisfied doing anything else besides writing fiction. Until that point, I thought my success in writing would be defined by the number of books I sold. After that point, it really didn't matter if my books sold. I just wanted to write and write well.

Of course, it wasn't very long afterwards that my writing career came to an abrupt halt and I returned to programming. But in the years since, I have tried to pay attention to the stories that move me to tears, to see if they are related and keep mental post-its on their essential elements.

(A side note: Those who study writing will tell you that there are a fixed number of original plots in the world. And there are many, many opinions regarding how many original plots there are and specifically what they are. But, the number of original plots isn't quite the focus of my investigation. I am specifically interested in the different ways that writers hit the moment.)

Presenting a definitive list is difficult because many of them overlap (for good reason, as we'll see in a moment). But here are a few themes that, at first glance, seem to be distinct:

Sacrifice: A soldier falls on a grenade to save the lives of his buddies. An old man donates a kidney to a little girl he has never met simply because he happens to be a match. A mother does without so her son can achieve his dream.

Validation: The high music teacher toils in obscurity but over the years writes a symphony in the hearts of his students. The pauper lives with the persistent sigh that he is more and eventually discovers his royalty. An unemployed single mother becomes a legal assistant and triumphs over a large utility company.

Reunion: A beloved son returns from war. Lovers are torn apart only to rekindle their love years later. A prodigal son realizes his mistake and makes the long journey home to welcoming arms.

Transcendence: The feisty boxer, who should be beaten, gets back up to fight again. A young girl, deaf and blind, becomes the first deaf-blind person to graduate from college and goes on to achieve world-fame as an author, activist and lecturer. A woman, upon learning that her ex-husband has contracted AIDS, moves back in with him to care for both him and his homosexual lover because both are dying from the disease.

Not long after I started the list, I realized that every major theme that evoked deep, yearning emotion in humans (i.e. every "archetype") could be found as facets of the redemption story of Christianity.

The redemption story shows us Jesus, who was God, coming to be born as a human, to live among us and to sacrifice himself for us.

The redemption story tells us of Jesus, a carpenter of no reputation, suddenly revealed as the Messiah and validated by the Holy Spirit. The redemption story also validates us as more than specks of dust on a dirt-ball of a plant. Instead it reveals us as sons and daughters of God.

The redemption story proclaims the great reunion of God and his beloved.

And the redemption story demonstrates transcendence through Jesus' death and resurrection and promises the same transcendence for us. No matter what our circumstance, it gives us the power to overcome.

There is a very good reason that every theme that moves us to tears inhabits some corner of redemption.

In Romans 8:19-23, Paul tells us that all of creation is yearning for the glory that will be revealed in us as sons and daughters of God. He says the creation was subjected to frustration but will be brought into glorious freedom and it groans for that day like a woman in the pains of childbirth. And he says that we groan as well, waiting eagerly for our adoption as sons, the redemption of our bodies.

In other words, there is a vibration throughout this planet and its inhabitants. It is a vibration that says there is something wrong with the world. It is a vibration that says that a profound change is approaching.

When we experience anything that resonates with that vibration, the vibration "amps up."

This is why writers can "hit the moment." Despite all our diversity in the human race, there are certain core vibrations that are common among us.

And it is no accident that those vibrations resonate in the Gospel of Jesus Christ.

serpents AND doves

In Matthew chapter 10, Jesus gives his disciples a few instructions before dispatching them to tell others that the kingdom of heaven is at hand.

In the middle of this commissioning, Jesus says that he is sending them out like "sheep among wolves" and he gives them this bit of advice in the latter part of verse 16 (NIV):

"...so be shrewd as serpents and innocent as doves."

(I grew up with the King James Version. I always quote this verse as "wise as serpents and harmless as doves" but "shrewd" and "innocent" have the better connotations.)

Not surprisingly, this bit of advice is an excellent approach to use with everyone you encounter in life. In fact, it is *the* reason that I usually get a checkmark beside the "Plays Well with Others" line item on my computer consulting grade card.

Before we delve into why this works, it might be good to broaden our understanding of what Jesus is saying.

The original Greek word for "shrewd" can also be interpreted, "intelligent," "wise" and "prudent." It communicates the idea of being mindful of one's interests.

The original Greek word for "innocent" can also be interpreted "simple" (and "harmless"). When used to describe wines and metals, it communicates the idea of being unmixed and pure. When used to describe mental activity, a similar idea applies: without a mixture of evil, free from guile.

With this in mind, let's review the basic premise of this book and see what happens when you interact with other humans.

If humans are in a constant internal struggle between flesh and spirit, and if the flesh within a person not only hates that person but every other human it encounters, it is inevitable that another person's flesh will—on occasion—gain the upper hand and cause an individual to do something to you that is specifically designed to hurt you and/or cause you frustration.

This should not surprise you.

Neither should it surprise you that the individual involved might be completely unaware this is happening.

Obviously, this kind of interaction can happen on a small, inconvenient level. It can also occur on a large, severe level.

Just as obviously, the trigger for the interaction might come from within you or it might be completely unprovoked (although the latter is somewhat rare).

So, the first step in "playing well with others" is to reduce the influence of the flesh in your own life. If you find yourself constantly getting into altercations with others, you might want to spend a bit of time on introspection.

But no matter how the conflict actually gets started, the best way out is to follow Jesus' advice. In other words, be mindful of the ways that a resolution to the situation can benefit you but don't allow your mind to filled with impurities like guile (i.e. don't embrace solutions that *only* benefit you and harm others).

This may sound like a lot to think about during an altercation. Especially, since the last thing the flesh wants you to do is think. But here's the technique that I use.

When I see the flesh rising up in another person, I "go to quiet." Then I start listening to my spirit, expecting the Divine to help me see a solution that will benefit everyone involved. Then I speak that solution, calmly, directly, to the other individual's spirit. I do this instead of immediately reacting to their flesh. (And, yes, there are special circumstances where this approach should be abandoned but let's stick with this for a few moments.)

The alternative to speaking directly to a person's spirit is to engage in an activity that—around the house—we call "pinging."

Pinging happens when you or another person's flesh riles up and causes a reaction from the other side of the altercation.

If you let your flesh "ping" off their flesh, their flesh will ping and then your flesh will ping and things will escalate. This is the flesh version of table tennis.

The only way to stop this game is to catch what the other individual's flesh throws at you and try to address the underlying beliefs that the flesh is using to stir them up. If you can get to those beliefs and dissipate them, you have an opportunity to reach the other individual's spirit and change the tone of the situation.

I have examples of this but I am going to pick one from a long time ago—one that doesn't even relate the point very well, one that I can barely remember. I'm going to do this because if I relate a story from anytime in recent years, someone might figure out who I'm talking about. (And even in the case of the individual whom I am about to discuss, I am sure that by this time in his life he has figured out a better way to relate to those around him. And, yes, I'm really hoping that this story happened like I remember it!)

I attended a K-12 school in the Philippines called Faith Academy with 500 other missionary kids. During my junior year I sang in the school's madrigal choir. One of the other members of the choir carried the nickname "Tank." I didn't know where the nickname came from. That was just what people called him.

After my junior year, the madrigal group flew to the United States and toured up and down the west coast for seven weeks, promoting the school. We spent a lot of time together. And as you can imagine, the flesh in all of us did its best to stir the pot on a few occasions.

As I recall, Tank had a knack for irritating people. While I hadn't yet worked my way through the ideas discussed at the beginning of this chapter, I was trying to govern my life using the notion of acting like I believed the Bible was true. Since the Bible recommended that I treat others with kindness, I tried to do that with everyone on the trip, including Tank.

At some point near the end of those seven weeks, Tank asked me if I knew how he got his nickname. When I replied that I didn't, he explained that, in elementary, he used to take up a position near the water cooler (i.e. the water tank) just before recess concluded. Then, as recess concluded, he would take a long drink of water so that no one else could. And, that's when the other kids christened him.

After he related that story, Tank thanked me for treating him with kindness even though he knew that he didn't always earn it.

The point is that Tank knew he did things to irritate people. He had a long history of it. But I got along fine with him because I was willing to treat him with kindness whether he "earned" it or not. I did this because I understood that it was in my best interest to attempt to cultivate a good relationship with everyone in the madrigal group (shrewd as a serpent) and because the entire group would benefit from as much unity as possible (innocent as a dove).

(And Tank? If you're reading this book and I've gotten this completely backwards and you never did anything like that in your life, I apologize and we'll just say that it happened in an alternate universe like the classic Star Trek episode, "Mirror, Mirror.")

Now, I realize that this is a trivial and inconsequential example but this serpent-and-dove methodology really does work on every scale. After all, Jesus gave his disciples this idea of serpents and doves just before he sent them out.

And what did he tell them to expect as they went out?

Trials, floggings, arrests, death and hatred. (Matthew 10:17-22)

If Jesus thought it would work for those things and if it worked for Tank, it will probably work for everything in between.

There is a special case in the serpent-and-dove approach that might not be readily apparent. In verse twenty-three, Jesus tells his disciples that when they are persecuted in one city, they should flee to the next.

In other words, sometimes it's just better to "get outta Dodge." In those cases, you really shouldn't try to speak directly to the spirit on the other side of the altercation, you should just leave. (And, the Divine will let you know when this is the better idea.)

To summarize: No matter what your provocation—or what your flesh tries to convince you is your provocation—letting the flesh run within you in the midst of an altercation never creates long-term benefit. It might give you a short-term rush. It might even gain you a short-term victory. But in every case, it will also give the flesh a foot-hold that your flesh will then attempt to use to create an environment of failure.

32:23

For me, the March 2008 sex-scandal involving former New York Governor Eliot Spitzer and a prostitute was just another chapter is an oft-rehearsed drama. The actual characters change with each act but the unraveling of lives and the destruction that follows remains completely predictable.

It's like watching a bad movie with an ending that you can guess in the first five minutes. The characters may seem gloriously happy, enjoying that picnic they've spread over the railroad tracks in the middle of a dark tunnel but everyone knows the train is coming.

Moses laid out the formula thousands of years ago.

As the Israelites prepared to cross the Jordon river and take possession of Palestine, some came to tell Moses that they wanted to stay on the east side of the river. The land was good. It had fortified cities. Seemed like a nice place to settle down.

They even offered to leave their wives and children behind and cross the Jordon with the rest of the Israelites. They pledged to help the rest of the Israelites until all had their rightful possession.

While not thrilled with the idea, Moses agrees and then utters one of the more famous phrases from the Torah. In Numbers 32:23, he tells them, in essence, "Okay, we'll try it your way. But if you fail, you can *be sure your sin will find you out.*"

In other words, if people are counting on you and you are failing them in some way and you are trying to keep it a secret, you can be certain that your failing will be revealed.

Take ex-governor Spitzer, for example. He is a family man. As a dedicated attorney general for New York, he built a political legacy on rooting out corruption. In his campaign to become governor he pledged to bring ethics reform to state government.

At some point, in the middle of all these obligations, he secretly begins visiting prostitutes. Obviously his flesh is driving him to do so to create an environment of failure.

It blinds him to the ridiculous fantasy that the "Emperor's Club VIP" is peddling: specializing in introductions of "fashion models, pageant winners and exquisite students, graduates and women of successful careers (finance, art, media etc...) to gentlemen of exceptional standards."

(A side note: the truth is that "Kristen" — Eliot Spitzer's "escort" — was a broken young lady, struggling to make ends meet as a musician, living with a boyfriend who paid her rent; a young lady who claims to have come from poor circumstances when investigations seem to show that she was raised in a 1.2 million dollar home.)

Certainly, the flesh in Eliot Spitzer could have stopped there. After all, the internal turmoil generated in the rift between his secret life, his family and his public personae would have been enough to cause him considerable torment.

But the flesh goes further. It also blinds him to the fact that he is vulnerable to the very techniques that he used in his investigations as attorney general. He sets up his liaisons using phones that he knows can be wiretapped. He pays for his liaisons using wire transfers that he knows can be traced.

And to top it off, the flesh apparently heckles him into contacting his bank to ask them to hide the source of the transfers...which, of course, raises suspicion.

Why does the flesh do this when it could have him behave in a stealthier manner and keep him in a psychological grinder for years?

Because it is *insuring* that he gets caught.

Because he's made promises.

Because he has obligations.

Because he has a family.

Because he has portrayed himself as a man of character.

Because his flesh wants to spew the widest possible arc of destruction.

Its goal is larger than Eliot Spitzer. It wants to destroy everyone connected with Eliot Spitzer.

It not only hates Eliot Spitzer. It hates his wife, his children and his associates. It wants to cause them as much pain, frustration and humiliation as it can.

It knows that if it does this, the flesh nature of all those other individuals will react and those individuals will probably allow themselves their fury. And it knows that each "allowance" advances the cause of destruction far beyond Eliot Spitzer.

Never forget that the flesh is an excellent tactician.

Be sure your sin will find you out.

the DIVINE discomfort

I am always intrigued by the notion that the Eternal should behave in a way that is comfortable to human imagination.

There is a television personality who has made a famous quote that the reason she began her drift from classic Christianity was because she heard a preacher describe God as "jealous" and she couldn't figure out why God would ever be jealous. So, she concluded that Christianity must contain falsehoods.

This is a theme that runs through many of the popular theologies of the day. In these theologies, the Divine is some amorphous, cloud of good will that exists to give humans whatever they want so long as they think the right thoughts or behave according to the appropriate patterns. Not surprising, the thoughts and patterns required in these cases are ones which humans find comfortable.

I could cite specific examples of this but I'm more interested in the cause than the symptoms.

The need to find God comfortable comes from a tactic of the flesh that I call "assuming in your own favor." As a general rule, if you find yourself quickly jumping to conclusions that always "pay" in your direction, you should re-evaluate them.

For instance, do any of these statements sound familiar?

"I'm sure they wouldn't mind doing that for us tomorrow."

"Oh, it's no problem if we get there late. I'm sure that happens all the time."

"Well, of course, they will be glad to help. That's what they get paid to do."

In each case the flesh is feeding you assurances that it has no way to substantiate. It does this, not because they are true but because the practice of parroting these kinds of assumptions will create the perception of a false little world within you. It is a world where everything revolves around you and the satisfying of your "needs." This increases your isolation and creates an environment of failure.

The same is true when we specifically "assume in our own favor" with regards to the Divine. If you are entirely comfortable with your definition of the Divine, it means that your flesh is entirely comfortable with your definition of the Divine. And that means the flesh has calculated at least part of the definition and it has elements that will lead to your failure.

Because of this, I expect the Divine to have mysteries I can't resolve. I expect the Divine to exhibit behaviors that make me wince.

My favorite analogy regarding the Divine discomfort comes from *The Lion, the Witch and the Wardrobe* by C.S. Lewis.

In one scene, the four human children come through the wardrobe into the land of Narnia and are befriended by Mr. and Mrs. Beaver. The Beavers describe Aslan, the true ruler of Narnia in glowing terms but at one point Mrs. Beaver finally mentions that Aslan is a lion.

The elder girl, Susan, reacts to this instantly and asks if Aslan is "safe." She observes that she will be nervous about meeting a lion.

You can almost hear the chuckle in Mrs. Beaver's voice as she replies that Susan definitely will be nervous. Then Mrs. Beaver says that if anyone can appear before Aslan without "their knees knocking, they're either braver than most or else just silly."

The younger girl, Lucy, doesn't appreciate this conclusion and presses for more clarity.

"Then he isn't safe?" she asks.

And with Mr. Beaver's response, C.S. Lewis makes the strongest statement I know regarding the Divine discomfort.

"Safe? Don't you hear what Mrs. Beaver tells you? Who said anything about safe? 'Course he isn't safe. But he's good. He's the King, I tell you."

scorched EARTH

For a time, I had one nagging question about the work of the flesh in my life. I had no problem believing that it hated me. I had no problem believing that it wanted to steal all that it could from me. I had no problem believing that it wanted to destroy all that was good in me.

But I struggled with the idea that it wanted to kill me.

Didn't the flesh have *any* notion of self-preservation?

Only recently have I realized that the flesh *can't* have a sense of self-preservation because the flesh has no future. When Jesus Christ died, it ended any chance that evil would ever truly triumph. Every force for evil in this world knows this and they are implementing the only tactic they have left.

They are engaged in a "scorched earth" policy. They know that Christ will return some day to establish his legitimate rule over the planet. In the mean time, they are going to try to burn to rubble everything beautiful that God has made.

So why then don't we have a world in full-scale rabid chaos, a world akin to the zombie movies with wolf-packs of homicidal maniacs charging through the streets devouring anyone they meet?

(At this point I should note that I am not unaware of the horrific atrocities that have occurred in the world, that are occurring in the world and will continue to occur in the world. I will comment on this in a few paragraphs but let me float a hypothesis first.)

In short, what keeps "all hell" from "breaking loose?"

In chapter two of Second Thessalonians, the Apostle Paul alludes to the fact that there is a force restraining the revelation of evil. I personally believe that God is limiting evil so that it cannot normally affect the physical world directly.

If that's true, every force for evil needs a human gateway to transition into the physical realm. And even when evil finds a useful human gateway, there is always the potential for the human who is under the influence to exercise his or her free will and stop evil's advance.

I know that Hollywood loves to give us movies about the supernatural intrusion of evil into our lives. But really, have you ever seen evil manifested that way in real life? Aren't you far more likely to see humans as the vehicles of hatred, death and destruction?

Here are the thoughts to ponder in all of this: *If* the evil in this world is absolutely committed to the utter annihilation of good but it must have the cooperation of humans to accomplish it, we can quickly reach two conclusions:

First, you cannot negotiate with the flesh. You can't appease it. You can't mollify it. If you indulge it, it will get stronger and take more from you. If you pet it, it will bite you. If you try to act like it doesn't exist, it will blind-side you. It is a terrorist. It is an "insurgent." It is relentless and single-focused and its entire existence is dedicated to your destruction and the destruction of everything around you because it has already lost.

Second, you as a member of the human race must choose, every moment of every day, to manifest good from the spirit or manifest evil from the flesh (and its helpers). And it will be one or the other.

Third, those humans that you feel so justified in despising? Those humans that perform atrocities going on in the world right now? The ones who murder, maim, rape and steal for whatever reason suits them at the time? You have exactly the same flesh within you as they have in them. Whether you are willing to admit it or not, under the right circumstance, you are capable of committing the same vile acts because the flesh within is utterly corrupt.

Unfortunately, it will be easy for you to slouch away from these conclusions because your flesh will whisper that you aren't currently running down the street with a rabid wolf-pack so you must be doing just fine.

In fact—while the flesh would love to turn you into its zombie—it usually operates in a far more subtle manner. It knows that it can't convince you to murder your spouse so it cajoles you into hissing criticisms instead. It knows it can't prod you into tossing your boss out the window so it tells you that you need to spend two hours a day at the office surfing the Internet because you need the stress relief.

In short the flesh will take whatever you allow it but everything you allow will be *unquestionably* dedicated in some way to your destruction.

the garage door

I tell you this story because it has all the elements of a flesh episode without actually looking like a flesh episode until the last moment.

A few weeks ago, I came home from work and pushed the button on my garage door remote control.

Nothing.

So, I pushed it again.

Nothing...again.

I got out of the car, walked into the house through the front door, circled into the garage and opened the garage door using the button on the wall. I noticed the light inside the button was flashing so after I pulled my car in, I headed for the Internet.

The manufacture's site said that the flashing light meant the remote wasn't programmed. In addition, a discussion board indicated that the unit in the garage had probably been hit by lightning and would need to be replaced.

I filed those pieces of information and went on with my evening.

In the morning, I opened the garage door from the button on the wall, hopped in my car, started to drive away and pushed the button on my garage door remote control.

Nothing.

Pushed it again.

Nothing.

So, I got out of my car, trotted back into the garage, pushed the button on the wall and scurried back to my car after very carefully hopping over the light beam at the base of the door. (It's a safety feature to stop the door from closing if there is a small child or animal in the way.)

I came home that evening and pushed the button on my garage door remote control.

Nothing.

Pushed it again.

Nothing.

Got out of my car. Walked in the front door, etc.

I did this for over a week. I'm a patient person. It wasn't really a problem. I had the problem on my list. I would get to it when I got to it. I'm the only person who uses that garage door and I'm a patient person because patience is a virtue and I'm a virtuous person...and very patient. (I trust you can hear the sarcasm in that paragraph.)

You should also know that I follow a system of organization in part based on "Getting Things Done" by David Allen. (If you have a difficult time keeping up with the elements of your life, I recommend it!)

One of David Allen's tenets is that if a task takes two minutes or less, you should not worry about trying to track it in your system, you should just do it. Because it will take longer than two minutes to put it into your system, manage it in your system and then get it back out of your system.

I knew that trying to reprogram the remote would most likely take under two minutes.

But I didn't do it.

I just kept walking around to the front door when I came home in the evening and I kept hopping "the light fantastic" when I left the next day.

Then one morning, I didn't quite clear the light beam and the door halted its descent and started back up.

"Grrrrrr!" the flesh erupted within me.

"Grrrrrr!" I parroted.

"Quick! Run back inside and try again," the flesh said.

I spun, bolted and rammed my head into the garage door because it was just out of my line of sight but not high enough for me to clear it without ducking.

At this point, holding my throbbing head, I started laughing because I knew exactly what had happened...

And I remembered that multiple times over the past few days, the spirit within had suggested that I reprogram the remote...

And I had listened to the flesh telling me that wouldn't do any good because lightning had hit the opener...

So instead of trying something constructive, I had spent the last week and a half jogging around the house...

Because I was so virtuous and patient.

Having realized all this, I suppose I could have let the flesh convince me that I should throw a little fit but it had already made a fool of me for days and I didn't see any point in continuing that ridiculousness.

When I arrived home that evening, I pushed the button on my garage door remote control.

Nothing.

I got out of the car. Walked around to the front door. Went to the closet. Got the tall step stool. Went out to the garage. Opened the door. Got the garage door remote control from my car. Reprogrammed it.

Reprogramming it immediately fixed the problem and it's been working ever since.

the talking STAIN

My all-time favorite commercial aired during Super Bowl 42 (February 2008). It promotes "Tide-to-go," a stain remover in a handy pen form factor.

(If, by chance, you haven't seen the commercial, you can find it on YouTube.com. Search for "talking stain ad". There have been a lot of take-offs on it so you might have to hunt a bit.)

The ad features a man dressed in white shirt and tie at a job interview. For the entire commercial, the man lists his job qualifications in his most earnest and sincere manner.

Unfortunately, there is a stain on the man's shirt. The man either does not realize he has a stain on his shirt or he has decided to act like it doesn't exist.

The stain has other plans. In fact, it is a talking stain and every time the man attempts some positive point about himself the stain interrupts with a line of gibberish that all but drowns out everything the man says.

Throughout the interview, the man's potential boss attempts to focus on the man. More often than not, however, the stain catches the boss's attention with its antics.

It is hysterical.

And it is one of the best illustrations that I've seen of the flesh.

This is exactly what the flesh does to us. It either convinces us that it doesn't exist. Or, it convinces us that what it's doing isn't a big deal.

Any time we try to accomplish anything, it does what it can to get in the way. And, even though it can be obvious to others that the flesh is making our lives miserable, it manages to hide in the blind spot that it has created for itself.

(I almost included this as just another example in the chapter "Truth Bubbles," but the commercial is so fabulous that I just had to give it its own chapter.)

So, what's the solution?

In the ad, it's easy. Remove the cap from Tide-To-Go. Take a few swipes and no more stain. And I'd love to tell you that the Tide-To-Go stain remover pen will work on the flesh as well but it's not that easy.

The stain of the flesh runs far deeper and you will contend with it in some form for the rest of your life. However, recognizing that the flesh exists and being able to identify its tactics is a great place to start in your quest to reduce its influence in your life.

And, if nothing else, maybe this analogy of the talking stain will help you become more aware of the schemes of the flesh in your own life.

the *quest*

"How do you justify your existence?"

Beginning in 1971, Isaac Asimov published a series of short stories about the Black Widowers, a group of men who would gather for dinner. Each time they would invite one guest who had a conundrum and the Black Widowers would attempt to solve it. I read some of those stories in high school and I can't remember the plots to any of them.

I do, however, recall the ritual that would always begin the interview of the guest. One of the Black Widowers would ask:

"How do you justify your existence?"

That question struck me. It wasn't the standard philosophical "Why am I here?" It was more like "Now that I'm here — and I'm consuming resources — what have I done and what am I doing to make myself worthy of the opportunity that life has given me?"

Certainly the tone of that question is far harsher than I would employ but there is an essence that I think it's good for us to consider.

Life is amazing. Our planet is a place of wonder, filled with resources that we have yet to understand — physical, mental and spiritual. Your mind is a treasure trove of possibilities. Every day you have the capability of making choices that will send ripples through countless other human beings.

No matter what your world view, it is a fact that your brain is the most advanced processing unit on the planet. Nothing else even comes close.

What will you do with that resource?

Whom will you influence?

Whom will you reflect?

What will you pursue?

What will you embrace?

What will you learn?

Whom will you teach?

What will be your epic?

What will be your quest?

Don't listen to the voice within you that says you'll never accomplish anything important. It's either trying to convince to devalue the important things that you are already doing or it's trying to keep you from recognizing your potential.

You're here.

Have an adventure!

Warning: The next two chapters examine the relationship between the flesh and male sexuality. These chapters are intended for a mature audience. (And, if you are wondering if this book contains a chapter on female sexuality, you may be disappointed or relieved to know that it does not. I am not qualified to write that chapter. I leave that to those who are.)

small TOOLS and flowers

(Note to the reader: This chapter is part one of a two part discussion on male sexuality. While it is not graphic, it *is* candid and plain-spoken. If you are offended by this topic, you should stop reading now and skip this chapter *and* the next.)

Some years ago, I met a Christian business associate. During the months that we worked together, we had many opportunities to share our experiences.

For a time, he worked with a company whose managers actually authorized the use of prostitutes by the staff during sales conventions. Obviously, my friend found this practice objectionable. Even worse, the managers told the staff that they could use their expense accounts to pay for these liaisons.

The managers instructed the staff to categorize the expense as "small tools or flowers."

This statement exposes a concept that I believe is the single most destructive lie that the flesh peddles regarding the relationships of men and women. I doubt this will come as any surprise to either men or women but—just to be obvious—I will state it anyway.

The belief is this: Women exist to help a man control his sperm count.

Put another way: Women are tools.

This concept permeates the world and it has caused incalculable destruction to men and women because it so completely corrupts the way men and women both conceptualize themselves and other men and women.

On a trivial level, this concept is the subtext for every commercial that uses women to catch a man's eye. The completely unsubtle message is that these women—or others like them—will be available to anyone who buys the product (i.e. drink the right kind of beer and you can have sex with a Swedish bikini team).

The concept is also the subtext for the majority of the performances by young women in the popular music industry.

"Don't cha wish your girlfriend was hot like me? Don't cha wish your girlfriend was a freak like me?" the Pussycat Dolls croon as they writhe through their music video. And, of course, several of the shots show the women with their mouths open and their tongues running over their teeth and lips.

Translation: "It's too bad that your girlfriend isn't like me because I'm willing to be used a tool anytime, anywhere."

(In truth, these are only performances. All of these entertainers go home at night and become real human beings — they are not sex machines, they are not "hot to trot" anytime, anywhere. If they are very fortunate, they have husbands who understand it is just an act. If they aren't, they get divorced. Just ask Joe DiMaggio or any of the other men who have married starlets or pop singers thinking their marriage bed would be just like the lie that is postulated by the performances.)

I could go on for pages citing examples but the more important question is: Why do I classify these examples as "trivial?"

Because it would be completely wrong-headed of us to look outward and identify "them" as the source of this corruption: those marketers, those music executives, those "playboys," those "hustlers."

As with everything else, the source of the problem isn't "out there," it is "in here." It is our comfort with the flesh-born lie that it is okay to conceptualize of half the human race as somehow less than human.

And lest you protest, asserting that you don't conceptualize of women as tools to help you control your sperm count, let me share a quaint story.

For a time, I served as interim music minister of my church. When I resigned, I wanted to remain at the church but I knew there would be comparisons with whomever led worship after me. Consequently, I "church-hopped" for several months to ease the transition.

One particular Sunday, I visited a near-by mega-church. As I recall, the pastor spoke from I Corinthians chapter eleven and he used the chapter as a springboard to launch into a discussion of propriety in worship.

For the final fifteen minutes of his sermon, he admonished the young women of his large congregation to dress more modestly. He even told them that if they didn't, they would be a distraction to the men during worship...and they certainly didn't want to be a distraction, did they?

The longer the admonition continued, the more I hoped the pastor would "flip the page" and address the problem from the opposite angle. I couldn't believe that he would conclude his sermon after targeting only the women in his congregation.

But he did.

I was stunned.

Aside from the fact, that he had just driven a psychological wedge through the middle of his congregation, he had — in essence — painted men as helpless slaves of their thoughts, unable to do anything but respond in a carnal manner when confronted with the female physique.

That kind of thinking puts women in burkas, covered from head to toe in heavy black fabric.

Yes, I understand that if you are a red-blooded male, you have most likely, at one point or another in your life, wished that one or more women would make themselves less attractive in some way so that you wouldn't experience a lustful thought.

But hold that thought for a moment and remember the central truth of the framework. *Everything* that proceeds out of your life, every thought, every word, every emotion and every action, *everything*, comes from flesh or spirit.

It is true that God has placed within you a profound appreciation of the female form. But honestly, do you believe the following thought pattern comes from flesh or spirit?

"Ooh, me like woman. Woman pretty. Me want woman. Me have sex with woman."

That thought pattern discounts any participation by the woman in the decision process because the underlying belief is that the woman is an object—a tool—to be used however and whenever the man wants.

The problem isn't the shape of a woman's body or the cloth that is draped around her body. The problem isn't even the lack of cloth draped around her body.

The problem is the belief that your flesh feeds your mind when confronted with those images. This is the point that Jesus was making when he said during the Sermon on the Mount that if a man lusts after a woman he has already committed adultery. He didn't say that you couldn't look at a woman and think, "Wow."

Unfortunately, the flesh is never going to stop pushing this belief that women are tools. Frankly, it is effective; it is destructive and most men will let it slide right into their brains without any resistance.

But, here's something you can try that should help. The next time you see an attractive woman and your flesh suggests that you could use her to control your sperm count, why not say a little prayer on her behalf, and even offer a bit of rejoicing?

"I thank you, my God, that you have placed such beauty in the world! I pray today that you would bless this lovely woman and make her a blessing to those around her. If she is a wife, I just ask that her husband would find his joy in her and she in him. If she is a mother, I pray that she will have your wisdom in raising her children so that when they are raised they themselves will 'rise up and call her blessed'. May she move from strength to strength today in whatever epic and quest that she has chosen. And at the end of the day, may she find her rest in you."

In other words, use the truth to push out the lies from the flesh.

What happens in your mind is your responsibility.

This is what I was waiting for the pastor of that large congregation to say. I just couldn't imagine that he wouldn't spend time admonishing the men of his congregation to exercise some discipline over their thought lives.

But, of course, he didn't. He just picked on the women.

My hope is that, maybe, just maybe, if we spend enough time living in the truth that women are human and deserving of every kindness and respect, the next time we see one of those open-mouthed supermodels on the television we'll think:

"That poor woman obviously has a bit of sinus congestion because she seems to be having difficulty breathing through her nose. She should try some nasal decongestant."

controlling the COUNT

(Note to the reader: This chapter is part two of a two part discussion on male sexuality. While it is not graphic, it *is* candid and plain-spoken. If you are offended by this topic, you should stop reading now.)

An indeterminate number of years ago, a wife wrote me with a question. (And yes, I am being purposefully vague.) She had discovered her early-adolescent son in his room masturbating to pornography. She wanted my opinion on what I thought she and her husband should do.

The question gave me a chance to formalize my thoughts on a topic that I had pondered for some time. It might be good to go through the process that I used to help you understand my final set of suggestions.

The first step I use in working toward an answer to any difficult question is to set boundaries using those things that I know are true.

The truth is that God is a good designer and that life is a result of his design. It is not haphazard or sporadic. Things that exist...exist for a purpose.

The truth is that I am a man and as a man, I am built to create sperm and release sperm. It is a complex, intricate process that engages a fantastic number of incredible molecular machines (see the chapter, "God of the Mundane").

The truth is that men and women have different designs. Even under completely healthy, normal circumstances, women—on average—do not have the same intensity of drive to participate in the sperm production and release cycle. (Not to mention there will be many times in even the best marriages when a woman will have no interest at all in this activity.)

The truth is that Jesus said that if a man looks on a woman with lust in his heart, it's the same as committing adultery with her. (My paraphrase of this verse would be that if you look at a woman and imagine using her as a tool to control your sperm count, it's the same as committing adultery with her.)

This is what I know to be true and it can set the boundaries of our discussion. From these truths, I would suggest to you that:

The sperm production process in men is a natural process. It is just like other bodily processes (i.e. eating, drinking and sleeping).

Just like any other bodily process, it can be abused. Over-eating can lead to gluttony. Over-drinking can lead to drunkenness. Over-sleeping can lead to ruin.

Just like any other bodily process, mismanagement has consequences.

Neglecting food causes hunger and eventual starvation.

Neglecting drink causes thirst and eventual desiccation.

Neglecting sleep causes fatigue and eventual psychosis.

(Yes, I am aware that Paul in 1 Corinthians 6:12-20 refutes those who equate sexual immorality with the normal process of eating. But the entire passage makes it very clear that Paul is talking about having intercourse with a prostitute — which is definitely *not* what I am going to propose in this chapter.)

Given that sperm production is a natural process designed by God, what process did God design for the facilitation of its release?

Unfortunately, in Christian circles, the standard answer is "marriage." Too often our young men and women are either directly taught or given the impression that a major cornerstone of any strong marriage is the wife doing her duty to help her husband control his sperm count.

To me, this idea seems contrary to some very basic principles of life.

First of all, if you are going to make a wife responsible for managing her husband's sperm count, are you going to extend that responsibility to his other biological needs? Is she responsible to feed him as well? Is she responsible to burp him? (I could follow this line to its logical end but I will defer.)

Second, stipulating that a wife bears *the* responsibility for her husband's sperm count turns her into a tool. (And I've already written an entire chapter on the problems with that idea.)

Third, not every man is married. If marriage is the only acceptable environment for sperm release then we should really go back to arranged marriages and pull kids out of school to marry them off as soon as they hit puberty because apparently that's what God had in mind when he designed us.

But, if marriage isn't the solution to facilitate sperm release for men, what is?

As already mention, visiting prostitutes is a bad idea. It doesn't matter if they get weekly health check-ups. Using a prostitute to control your sperm count solidifies the idea that women exist for this purpose.

Masturbating to pornography is a bad idea. It creates an appetite in your system that will eventually consume you. And, it objectifies women in your mind and causes you to classify them only as tools to control your sperm count.

Starting to see a pattern here? All these approaches to sperm release—marriage, prostitution, pornography—share a common thread. It is the same thread that I discussed in the previous chapter on male sexuality. It is one of the most destructive lies that the flesh peddles in our lives: That women exist to help a man control his sperm count.

What's the alternative?

Men should take responsibility for their own sperm count.

As far as I know, the Bible never directly addresses the topic of a man "controlling his sperm count." (And from this point forward, I am going to use this terminology to abstract the activity because the term masturbation carries a heavy connotation.)

(Note: There is a story in Genesis 38:8-10 about a man named Onan who was put to death because he "spilled his semen on the ground." But Onan wasn't put to death because he controlled his sperm count; he was put to death because he was refusing to fulfill his filial obligations. His brother Er had died and — in that culture — it was Onan's responsibility to father a child with Er's wife so that Er's lineage could continue.)

And what is the general reaction in our society to a man controlling his sperm count?

Disgust, embarrassment, ridicule, criticism, shock, guilt, shame, etc.

Do these reactions originate from the spirit or from the flesh? (In case you don't recognize the rhetorical nature of that question, I will answer! They originate from the flesh.)

Why would the flesh — and the collection of flesh which makes up the "world" — expend this much negative energy on this issue?

Because the flesh wants us to shun the obvious solution. Because shunning the obvious solution creates noise in our systems. Because shunning the obvious solution drives us to behavior that creates an environment of failure.

How many men have destroyed their lives and marriages because they refused to take responsibility for their own sperm count?

How many women have destroyed their lives and marriages because they mistook a man's need to use them as a tool for genuine affection?

Here's what happens when you don't manage your sperm count.

As your sperm count increases, your body will start releasing hormones to let your brain know that it's time to decrease the count. This will create a buzz in your brain and cause your thoughts to continually drift towards sex.

If you ignore these messages, and continue to let your count increase, your brain will begin tagging your visual input. Every image will be graded in terms of its suitability for use as a tool to reduce your count. And your flesh will suggest a myriad of places for you to find images that have a high level of suitability.

And eventually, if you continue to let your count increase, you brain will take control of your systems while you are asleep and reduce the count for you. (But, by the time this occurs, you will have subjected yourself to a great deal of frustration and noise.)

On the other hand, if you consistently control your count, you will find that you are able to look women in the eye and talk to them as individuals (provided you actively deny the lie that women are tools).

If you consistently control your count, you will find that the atmosphere of your life will grow calmer.

And, you may find that certain ideas that previously found traction in your mind suddenly have less traction. ("Go to some skanky part of town to meet with a woman I don't even know and pay her money to do something I can easily do myself?! Are you kidding me? Why would I ever do that?!")

Yes, there is potential for abuse here. But there is potential for abuse in everything we do.

So, here's the essence of what I suggested (along with some additional thoughts I've added in the mean time) to the wife who had discovered her son masturbating to pornography:

Explain to him how his body works, especially the relationship of hormones and sperm count.

Advise him that the enemies of his soul will attempt to use this to enslave him.

Help him understand that pornography is a trap.

Warn him that his flesh will attempt to convince him that women exist solely to help him control his sperm count.

Suggest that while sexual intercourse with a committed spouse is a beautiful and wonderful adventure, his sperm count is and will remain his responsibility for the rest of his life.

Notice: This concludes our discussion of the relationship of the flesh and male sexuality. We now return to our normally scheduled programming.

life in the Big house

Often, as I share my life with others, we discuss the connection between truth and freedom. At some point, someone will quote the verse from John chapter 8 where Jesus says, "...you will know the truth and the truth will set you free." (NIV)

It's unfortunate, that Jesus' statement doesn't have the same impact that it did thousands of years ago. Cultures change. Connotations drift.

To get the gist of what Jesus was really saying in this verse, it helps to look at the reactions of those on the other side of the conversation.

The story begins in John 8, verse 31. Jesus starts a conversation with those who believe that he is the Messiah.

"If you hold to my teachings," he says, "you are really my disciples. Then you will know the truth, and the truth will set you free." (NIV)

These statements raise an immediate objection in the believers because the word "free" had a different context than it holds today. At that time, calling someone "free" meant that they weren't a slave.

The reverse was also true. Implying that someone wasn't free meant that you had identified them as a slave (and no one wanted to be a slave).

Just for the sake of clarity, let me point out again that Jesus is speaking to those who already believe in him and he has just said that in order to truly be his disciples they need to hold to his teaching and only *then* will they be free.

Verse 33 of John 8 records their reaction. "They answered him, 'We are Abraham's descendants and have never been slaves of anyone. How can you say that we shall be set free?'" (NIV)

Over their objections, Jesus elaborates in the next verses: "I tell you the truth, everyone who sins is a slave to sin. Now a slave has no permanent place in the family, but a son belongs to it forever. So if the Son sets you free, you will be free indeed." (NIV)

When Jesus talks about the family, the image that comes to my mind is the "big house," a massive mansion with beautiful lawns, acres of vineyards and vast crop-bearing fields.

Jesus indicates there are two groups living in this house. There are the sons and daughters of God. And there are the slaves.

But the slaves aren't slaves because God made them slaves. The slaves are slaves because they choose to remain slaves. They have every opportunity to be sons and daughters. Instead, they "sin" and remain in slavery.

Unfortunately, the word "sin" is one of those words that we brush aside with ease because the flesh within us likes to push the definition of "sin" to actions that we can easily deny. We don't murder. We don't commit adultery. Therefore, we don't "sin."

But, Jesus doesn't afford us such comfort. His definition of sin isn't just external. We may not murder someone but are we enraged? We may not have an illicit affair but do we lust?

From this perspective, it's easy to see the truth in Jesus' statement regarding the connection of sin to slavery. If you allow yourself to be enraged or lustful, it will become easier to be enraged or lustful and soon you will be enslaved.

And isn't that true of other mental processes? If you worry, your life will soon be consumed by worry. If you judge, your life will soon be consumed with judgment.

Perhaps, this is why Jesus looked at those who believed in him and admonished them to "hold" to his teachings and "know" the truth. Perhaps he could see the bondage within them.

But, here again, the flesh within us tends to dilute the commitment and depth of those two words. Saying that you are going to "hold" to what Jesus commands (in the Sermon on the Mount, for instance) is far different than actually practicing it.

In fact, Jesus highlighted this difference in another parable that dealt with "son-ship."

In Matthew 21:28-32, Jesus tells a story about a man with two sons. The father asks each to work in his vineyard. The first says he won't and storms out. But then, he recants and does. The second readily agrees to work in the vineyard. He then smiles, strolls out and promptly "forgets."

Jesus concludes with "Which of the two did what his father wanted?" (NIV)

The obvious answer is the one who worked in the vineyard...even though he said he wasn't going to do it.

The principle is this: When the words that come out of your mouth don't match your practice, your practice counts.

Apparently, this was the problem with the believers that Jesus admonished at the beginning of this chapter. They had the right profession; they just didn't have the right thoughts and actions. (To use my terminology, they were following the beliefs that their flesh was peddling as opposed to the beliefs that the spirit was whispering.)

Want something else to ponder?

Why not broaden our categorization a bit? We've been discussing slaves and sons in the context of those who believe in Jesus but the truth is that every human on earth is loved by God. Everyone one of us—at a fundamental level—is a son or daughter of the Divine.

For a moment, let's extend the idea of the big house to this entire world and think about the fact that across humanity there are slaves and sons (and daughters).

Those who practice what Jesus teaches find some measure of freedom. Those who shun lust will find freedom from lust. Those who shun rage will find freedom from rage. The same holds true for worry and judgment.

Those who don't practice what Jesus teaches will find themselves enslaved — whether or not they pay lip-service to Jesus Christ as their Savior.

(Note: I am not saying that I believe that full "sonship" can be attained through action alone. I do believe in the "profession of faith." But, we rob ourselves of the fullness that the earth-bound Christian life has to offer if we stop there.)

a third PIVOT

As I've already said, I mark two major pivot points in my life. The first came when I was young and I wondered what it would be like if someone acted as if he or she believed the Bible was true. The second came with a whisper that revealed the flesh as a dedicated, scheming foe.

I also mentioned that I suspected there will be a third in my quest to understand how life works.

I suspect this because there is a boundary I have yet to cross and Jesus gave us every indication that we could, should and would cross it.

If you read the Gospels at face value, you find Jesus constantly operating at a supernatural level. It was like air to him: Heal the sick, raise the dead; walk on water; feed thousands with a single meal, tell the Pharisees what they are thinking. None of it seems to require much effort. (Yes, Jesus does sense when healing flows out of him but it doesn't seem to sap his energy.)

And Jesus tells his disciples, among other things, that they will do greater works than he has done.

In this context, one particular miracle fascinates me.

(Note: Before going any further, I should tell you that this is not a chapter with answers, just observations.)

Towards the end of his time on earth, Jesus rides into Jerusalem on a donkey. Crowds gather to wave palm branches and celebrate. That night Jesus returns to Bethany to rest. The next day Jesus makes the trip back to Jerusalem. He sees a fig tree. It has lots of leaves—normally, a sign of fruit—even though it isn't the season for fruit.

Jesus walks up to the fig tree, finds it empty, and curses it. The tree dies.

Now, I know that there are many who have offered a variety of interpretations regarding the point Jesus was trying to make during this incident but I will guarantee you that the disciples focused on one and only one thing. (And honestly, it's the thing that caught my attention.) In fact, I would venture to say that Jesus knew that this one thing would be the showstopper. And pretty much anything he said after the showstopper would turn into "blah, blah, blah, blah" (unless he upped the ante). Because—with a bit a paraphrasing—this was the *only* thing bouncing around in the brains of the disciples after the showstopper:

"Dude! He just cursed a tree and it *died*. He *cursed* the tree and, D-E-D, dead! How awesome is that?"

As far as I'm concerned if Jesus was trying to make some great theological or prophetical point, he should have made it *before* he nuked the tree.

But Jesus didn't do that. In fact, in the midst of the disciples' astonishment, Jesus casually remarks that—if they have faith—they will not only be able to give trees the proverbial "stink eye," but they will be able to tell a mountain to throw itself into the sea.

Again, if Jesus is trying to make some statement beyond the obvious, he's not doing a very good job because it sure sounds to me like Jesus is telling us that if you are a person of faith, the laws of the known universe are flexible.

This makes sense.

God made and maintains the universe. He hears the requests of his children. The Bible tells us that faith pleases him. Who's to say that God hasn't built certain engines into the world that are only engaged through faith?

So…why don't we find the universe flexible?

Sometimes, when I discuss this with others over a meal, I pause at this point and then facetiously observe, "Personally? I think the problem is with God." And, yes, I could dedicate several paragraphs to the standard excuses that we use to justify our rigid existence but I don't find any of them convincing.

On the other hand, there have been moments in my life when I have slipped into the supernatural but they aren't what you might expect.

Several years back, I received a phone call from my mom.

"Philip!" she said. "We just bought a car. Guess what kind of car we bought."

And I said, "Mom, you bought a Lincoln-Continental."

"Oh," she exclaimed, "how did you know that?"

"You just had that Lincoln-Continental sound in your voice, mom," I joked.

I can tell you emphatically, this was not a guess. And it was different than a whisper. It was knowledge. I knew…as if I had access to the answer in her brain.

I could tell you other stories but I'm trying to keep this chapter short.

It doesn't happen all the time. I can never predict when it's going to happen. And, sometimes, when I would like it to happen, it doesn't.

I've come to wonder if faith is "digital."

As I write this (in November 2008), the United States is making final preparations for the conversion to digital television. As I've learned from the frustrating experience of trying to make the switch sooner rather than later, digital television is not like analog.

We live about twenty miles from the television towers that service Springfield, Missouri. We live in the country, surrounded by hills and trees.

In the days of analog television, I put an antenna in my attic, bought a cheap amplifier and life was grand. If I had a station that didn't come in as clear as the others, it wasn't really a problem. Sure, it had a little snow but the picture was still there. The audio was still there.

Digital television is different. Even with my antenna mounted on my roof and a more expensive amplifier, it doesn't always work. And when I say, it doesn't work, I mean it doesn't work.

Digital television has three basic states. Either the picture is beautiful. Or it is pixelating (that's when boxes start appearing randomly on the screen). Or…it's off.

In digital, there is a threshold. It doesn't matter how close you are to the threshold, when you're below it, you have no picture. When you're above it, all is beautiful.

And when you're right on threshold and you are almost "on", things are scattered. One moment, there's picture. One moment, there are boxes on the screen. Then, there's no picture.

My dance with the supernatural is like that. While I enjoy a whispered communication with God every day, every once in a while, I slip across the threshold and see that there's more.

And then I slip back.

This "pixelating" doesn't really discourage me. I know God loves me and I'm crazy about him. And I know that I'm on a journey with him and someday I'll understand things better.

But, I have to admit that there are times when I wish that I already understood things better: When friends are holding firm in the midst of pending sorrow and they are praying and I am praying with them. In those instances, it would be wonderful to flex the rules of the universe a bit.

Certainly, it would be easy to resign myself to the "Will of the Divine" when certain prayers aren't answered. And I have taken refuge there on many occasions.

But, to be honest, there is a whisper within me that hints—without shame, without condemnation, without guilt— that there's more.

Why would the Divine grant me access to something as trivial as knowing the kind of car my parents bought and then deny me access to that which seems far more important?

I don't think he does.

I think the problem is with me. And, frankly, I think I'm making it harder than it is.

Yes, the miraculous only happens within the "will" of God. On the other hand, the will of God may be far more vast and deep and delightful and whimsical and mischievous than we think.

And he may even be "willing" to let those who don't call themselves Christians operate the engine of faith. It would explain a few of the mysteries that I find in the world.

As for me, I keep listening. I keep loving. I keep watching and learning.

And when I hit the third pivot? I'll let you know. I trust you'll do the same for me!

truth BUBBLES

I love listening for Jesus in the nooks and crannies of human experience.

If it's true—as Paul says in Colossians—that Jesus is the one who holds everything together, it's also true that he is intimately connected to all reality;

And if it's true that he is the Way, the Truth and the Life (as he claimed in John chapter 14);

Then it seems like we should be to find him "bubbling" into our world, especially since Paul tells us that Jesus has already reconciled the entire world to himself through his sacrifice. If there is no enmity between him and his creation, why wouldn't he allow his essence to slip into the world?

For instance, I remember smiling after the men's 4 X 100 freestyle relay at the Bejing 2008 Olympics.

Not because the Americans beat the French.

Not because I knew it put Michael Phelps in the running to break the all-time individual gold medal record for a single Olympic games.

But because of what Jason Lezak said after the race.

A bit of background: The French team was favored to win. On the anchor leg, Jason Lezak—the oldest member of the team—was swimming against Frenchman Alain Bernard. Alain Bernard began the race as the world-record holder in the 100 meter freestyle. And Alain Bernard had a head start.

When the swimmers flipped at the 50 meter mark, Alain Bernard was a half-a-body ahead. Did I mention he was the world-record holder?

Listen to what Jason Lezak says about this moment after the race.

"I'm not going to lie. When I flipped at the 50 and saw how far ahead he was, I thought, 'No way.' Then it changed. It's the Olympics. It's for the USA. I got a super charge and took it from there."

Jason Lezak not only caught and passed the world-record holder, he set a new world record.

What happened? Jason Lezak's flesh tried to get him to quit but Jesus nudged him:

"Try."

No, Jesus doesn't love Americans more than the French but when someone responds to the voice of the Eternal instead of the voice of their flesh, extraordinary things can happen.

And what about all those wonderful sayings that crop up all over the world? Those sayings that whisper "truth" when you hear them even though they come from the lips of those who have entirely different world views from ours?

I once heard a Buddhist priest say, "The source of all your suffering is self."

That's good. And that's true.

I once read a quote by a Native American Shaman named Little Joe. "Worrying is praying for what you don't want."

That's good.

The Bhagavad Gita says, "Hell has three gates: lust, anger, and greed."

There's truth in that.

And then there's the Tao: "A virtuous life is lived as water — flowing easily; moving away from resistance or collision; always delicate, graceful, and calm."

But...I would expect to find some truth in other systems of belief. After all, the individuals who start belief systems usually spend some time observing life and, if you observe life for long enough, you pick up on the principles that are pressing into it from eternity.

It's far more fun for me to dig truth out of contemporary culture. I suppose my mom popularized this sport for me.

When I was growing up in the Philippines, *Star Trek* was the only television show she would watch with the rest of the family. And every week, she would find a "spiritual application."

I remember wrinkling my nose at this when I was growing up. But now, I do it too!

There's scene from *The Matrix* that I love.

A bit of background: The movie *The Matrix* is science fiction and it is set in a future where machines have created a virtual world to imprison humans. The humans are living their lives in this fake world but it's all just happening in their minds while their bodies are producing heat to power the machines.

Fortunately, there is a resistance movement—a group of humans who have broken free of the virtual world and now live in the real world. These resistance fighters often venture back into the virtual world to help other humans break free.

The "Oracle", on the other hand, works within the system. In one scene, the film's messianic character, "Neo," goes to see the Oracle. As he waits in the outer room, he watches an Indian child bending spoons.

With a curious smile the Indian child hands Neo a spoon and says, "Do not try to bend the spoon; that's impossible. Instead, only try to realize the truth."

Neo asks, "What truth?"

And the boy responds, "There is no spoon."

Neo replies, "There is no spoon?"

The boy continues, "Then you will see, it is not the spoon that bends, it is only yourself."

In other words, the boy's ability to behave in a manner that is fundamentally different comes from understanding the truth of his existence, not from struggling to overcome the deceit of his existence.

Though the boy can see the spoon, though the boy can feel the spoon, the boy knows that the spoon and all his surroundings are merely a virtual world created by the machines. Since everything he sees is a deception there is no reason for him to be rigidly bound by it and he bends himself in the way he chooses.

Here's the spiritual application: Your flesh will try its best to convince you that the life that it has crafted for you is your life—that its tantrums, its desires, its anger, its despair all belong to you.

But God has already defeated the flesh and the war is over. All that remains is an illusion that only has the power that you give it.

If you want something different in your life, you can begin to embrace it at any time by realizing this truth. In other words, "There is no spoon."

That's good. I like it.

I say all this to say: Don't be surprised if you look into another philosophical backyard and find truth bubbling up like black gold from the ground. Jesus is everywhere and he loves everyone. Of course, his truth is going to turn up in other worldviews.

And anytime, anyone, anywhere operates in some measure of the truth that is everywhere in the world, he or she will succeed in some fashion.

schizophrenia

As I chat with friends about the flesh and the spirit, I can generally group individuals into two camps: those who cling to their "integrity" and those who are willing to become "schizophrenic."

The first group tends to say things like this:

"It's just the way I feel. I can't change the way I feel."

"I was angry when I heard that I didn't get the promotion."

"I'm so frustrated I could just spit."

"I'm going to go down there and give those people a piece of my mind."

"They hurt my feelings because of what they said."

"I can't do it. I just can't."

The flesh loves these kinds of statement because, in every case, it has initiated the beliefs that drive the emotions which in turn drive these statements. But it has hidden itself so well that the human who is in the process of erupting truly believes that he or she is the source of the emotion.

Of course the flesh can prompt us to more than just emotion. As already mentioned, it can drive our thoughts, words and actions. In all cases, however, the person who chooses the path of self-integrity allows the flesh to operate very efficiently because the individual will believe that everything they experience internally comes from a single source: the "me."

The "me" is a useful construct for the flesh because – as long as it remains in place – the flesh can generate a wide variety of undesirable consequences in its host and the host will continually place the blame everywhere except the flesh.

When I was growing up in the Philippines, one of my friends had a small tree monkey for a pet. Some tree monkeys have a peculiar way of greeting you and figuring out if you are a friend or an enemy.

The first time they see you...they charge! And, before you know it, they have run up your leg and are sinking their teeth into your neck. Not hard, just enough so that they know that you know that they could do some damage if they took a real bite.

At that moment, you have a choice. You can scream, rip the monkey from your neck, sling it at the back wall and run in the other direction like a mad man. (Bear in mind: The monkey will *never* forget that you did this.)

Or you can pet the monkey, talk softly to it and in a few moments it will release your neck and you'll be friends. You've passed the test. It knows you aren't afraid of it.

So my friend had this monkey and I had successfully passed the initiation ritual but our mutual buddy from next door hadn't. That meant that he and the monkey were enemies for life.

One day, my friend tells me that he wants to show me something funny so we sneak around to the back of his house where he keeps his monkey. He creeps up to the monkey — who is sound asleep in a little tree — and my friend suddenly hollers as loud as he can mere inches from the monkey's face.

In a split-second, the monkey goes from blissful slumber to stark, raving terror; screaming and scrambling backward up the tree as fast as it can.

My friend thinks this is the funniest thing in the world and I have to admit that the look on that monkey's face was something I will never forget — and I thought it was pretty funny too.

But then the monkey did something that made me laugh even harder. After a few moments, the monkey regained enough of its composure that it was ready to seek some vengeance for its rude awakening. Thus composed, it started looking for an enemy.

It looked at my friend...and decided he wasn't the enemy.

It looked at me...and decided I wasn't the enemy.

And then it saw my buddy from next door who was standing all the way over near the corner of the house—an impossible distance, far too far away to be responsible.

But, since my buddy from next door was the only enemy in sight, the monkey concluded that he did the deed and it immediately started hissing at him and baring its teeth.

My buddy from next door didn't appreciate the accusation but my friend and I thought it was hilarious.

This is what it's like when someone lives with a concept of self-integrity. That person, like the monkey, looks at the flesh—the entity that is truly responsible for whatever distress he or she is enduring—and dismisses the idea that the flesh is responsible. Instead the person focuses on whomever the flesh accuses even though the accused might not have had any roll in the deed at all.

(As a father, have you ever blamed your kids for taking your tools when you are the one who lost them in the first place?)

On the other hand, some of us have chosen a kind of schizophrenia. Not in the clinical sense but in the literal. Schizophrenia literally means "a splitting of the mind". It can also mean a condition resulting from the coexistence of antagonistic identities.

The Apostle Paul gives the most famous Biblical discussion of this in Romans 7. We pick up the passage with verse 18 (NIV):

"I know that nothing good lives in me, that is, in my sinful nature. For I have the desire to do what is good, but I cannot carry it out. For what I do is not the good I want to do; no, the evil I do not want to do—this I keep on doing. Now if I do what I do not want to do, it is no longer I who do it, but it is sin living in me that does it. So I find this law at work: When I want to do good, evil is right there with me. For in my inner being I delight in God's law; but I see another law at work in the members of my body, waging war against the law of my mind and making me a prisoner of the law of sin at work within my members. What a wretched man I am! Who will rescue me from this body of death? Thanks be to God — through Jesus Christ our Lord! So then, I myself in my mind am a slave to God's law, but in the sinful nature a slave to the law of sin."

That sounds fairly schizophrenic to me!

Paul continues this objectification of the sinful nature (i.e. the carnal nature, the flesh, the old man) in many other passages. For instance, Paul gives an extensive comparison of living by the spirit versus living by the sinful nature in Galations 5:16-26. It is the passage that begins,

"So I say, live by the Spirit, and you will not gratify the desires of the sinful nature. For the sinful nature desires what is contrary to the Spirit, and the Spirit what is contrary to the sinful nature. They are in conflict with each other, so that you do not do what you want." (NIV)

And don't we have a long tradition in our culture of the idea that an angel rests on one shoulder and a devil on the other? Granted, cultural conceptions are a lousy place to find your worldview but isn't it interesting that this idea of warring entities within us pervades our consciousness?

The advantage of adopting the schizophrenic mindset is that you can disconnect yourself from the activity of the flesh and consider it objectively instead of simply reacting to every belief it pushes at you.

And that millisecond of pause may be just enough for you to hear the voice of another within you—a voice that truly desires the best in your life instead of continually scheming over your destruction.

In other words, be the human, not the monkey.

the Fortress of ANGER

How ferociously we protect our anger.

Though we disavow most other negative emotions, we have built a wall around this one, carefully aligning its boundaries to the favored proof-text—the cornerstone that we quote over and over to justify our behavior whenever we want to have a flesh-fit.

We say, "Well, the Bible says, 'Be angry and sin not, let not the sun go down on your wrath.' That means you can be angry without sinning. You just have to make sure that you're not angry by the time you go to sleep."

Of late, whenever I hear someone quote this verse, I can almost see the Apostle Paul up in heaven rolling his eyes. Because...if you'll just take a bit of time to correlate this scripture with other passages from the epistles and examine the context, you will find that Paul might not be giving us a pass to throw a tantrum any time we want...as long as it is during the day.

For instance, our proof-text comes from Ephesians 4:26 but what about Ephesians 4:31? A mere five verses later Paul says, "Get rid of all bitterness, rage and anger, brawling and slander, along with every form of malice." (NIV)

As you can see, Paul groups anger with "a lotta other ugly" and tells us to get rid of it.

In Colossians 3:8 (NIV) Paul says, "But now you must rid yourself of all such things as these: anger, rage, malice, slander, and filthy language from your lips."

And, Paul tells the Corinthians that he's hesitant to come to them because he may not find them as he wants them to be. He says he fears that there may be "quarreling, jealousy, outbursts of anger, factions, slander, gossip, arrogance and disorder." (2 Corinthians 12:20 NIV)

Paul also writes to Timothy and says that he wants "men everywhere to lift up holy hands in prayer, without anger or disputing." (1 Timothy 2:8 NIV)

And what about James? He tells us in chapter one verses 19-20, "My dear brothers, take note of this: Everyone should be quick to listen, slow to speak and slow to become angry for man's anger does not bring about the righteous life that God desires." (NIV)

In fact, if you look at the context of our proof-text, you will see that the entire section—verses 17-32—deals with abandoning the attitudes and practices of the old self and embracing the attitudes of the new self (or abandoning the flesh and embracing the spirit). It deals with moving away from bitterness, rage, anger, brawling and slander and moving toward kindness, compassion and forgiveness.

And if you step away from the proof-text for a minute and slip it into those themes, it isn't that far removed from them. When the Apostle Paul says, "Be angry and sin not, let not the sun go down on your wrath," the focus is on moving *away* from anger. He even adds the postscript, "Neither give place to the devil." The clear implication is that dwelling in anger gives the devil a foothold in your life and the Apostle Paul doesn't want to see that happen.

Even more interesting to me is that some translations cross reference this verse back to Psalms 4:4. It's easy to understand why when you read the New International Version's translation of the psalm: "In your anger, do not sin; when you are on your beds, search your hearts and be silent."

However, there is a wide variety of translations for Psalms 4:4. For instance, the New American Standard translates Psalm 4:4 this way, "Tremble and do not sin; Meditate in your heart upon your bed, and be still."

The Amplified Bible gives an alternate translation of "stand in awe and sin not."

Here's the problem: the Hebrew word in this case has a range of meanings and is translated in many different ways: "come trembling," "deeply moved," "disturbed," "enraged," "excited," "moved," "provoke," "quake," "quarrel," "rages," "shakes," "stirred," "tremble," "troubled," "turmoil."

My paraphrase of Psalm 4:4 is this: "When you are emotionally distressed, don't sin. Get quiet and meditate on God."

So why did Paul pick the word "angry"? Well, the Septuagint—an early Greek translation of the Old Testament—uses "angry" in Psalm 4:4. The verse might have been in common enough usage at the time that Paul is quoting it as something that will be familiar to his readers. Or, Paul might be remembering the verse from the original Hebrew and transliterating into Greek himself. If it was the latter, I'm sure that Paul understood the nuances of the Hebrew.

Either way much is lost in the translation when moving from the Hebrew to the Greek because in Greek the word just means anger. Losing this kind of subtlety is a common problem because there is rarely one-to-one correlation in languages.

Of course, ever since, the flesh in all of us has lifted this verse out of context, highlighted the word "angry", put it in a box and used it as a cornerstone to build a fortress around every temper tantrum, hissy-fit, outburst and conniption that it wants to throw.

It has deluded us into believing that *some* anger is okay. (And certainly, if you can find a way to label it "righteous indignation"…well…that can give you *carte blanch* to act any way you want.)

In reality, however, anger is rarely righteous and it is rarely beneficial. It creates noise in your system. It makes it more difficult to hear the voice of the Spirit within you. And because of that it blinds you to the best course of action in your immediate situation.

So how should we deal with anger when it rises? The same way we deal with every ploy of the flesh: Get quiet and let the Spirit help you understand the lie that the flesh is feeding you to disturb your peace. Remember that every emotion is based on a belief. If you can expose that belief, you can determine if the belief is true or false and when you oppose a false belief with truth, the anger will evaporate.

Not surprisingly, this is very similar to the approach suggested in Psalm 4:4 (if you choose to translate the Hebrew word as "anger").

welcome BACK to the broadcast

As I mention in other chapters, for years I have focused on personal interactions as the primary way to grow and help others grow in the life of abundance. As I say elsewhere, I have never been anti-church. Church is wonderful for a joint worship experience and a dynamic speaker can certainly provide food for thought. I just think that discipleship happens at a different ratio. Real growth requires intimate tending.

I will admit, however, that I have been too narrowly focused on personal interactions as *the* method for achieving abundance. And, because of that the Holy Spirit had to whisper a reminder to me as I drove home from work.

"You know," he began with a smile, "Jesus *did* tell the parable of the sower."

I nodded...immediately recognizing that God has many ways to "grow" his children.

"Welcome back to the broadcast," a whisper snickered within me.

For those of you who might not know, the term "broadcast" originally meant exactly like it sounds. It was a way to cast (i.e. to throw) seed in a broad (i.e. wide) pattern. A farmer would shoulder a bag of seed and—as he walked through a field—he would take a handful of seed and "broadcast" it outward in a large arc.

Jesus picked up this activity and used it in one of his most famous parables. As always we can learn the most by not only considering the parable but the context as well and the conversations that follow it.

The parable of the sower occurs at the beginning of Matthew 13 and Luke 8. We'll focus on the passage from Matthew.

A large crowd gathers.

Jesus tells a simple parable: A farmer goes out to sow his seed. As he broadcasts it, some falls on a path, some falls in rocky ground, some falls among thorns and some falls on good ground. The seed on the path is eaten by birds. The seed on the rocky ground grows quickly but dies in the heat because the roots are shallow. The seed among the thorns is choked to death. Only the seed that falls on good ground flourishes and produces a good crop.

Jesus concludes the parable with, "He who has ears, let him hear." (NIV)

Afterwards, the disciples come and ask Jesus why he speaks to the crowd in parables.

Jesus replies, "This is why I speak to them in parables: Though seeing, they do not see; through hearing, they do not hear or understand." (NIV)

I know that Jesus is quoting from Isaiah chapter 6 and is indicating that his activity is a fulfillment of prophecy. Still, this certainly isn't what we would consider the normal attitude for a teacher who is trying to recruit followers.

Jesus tells a few stories. If people can figure out what he's trying to say, fine. If they don't get it, well…too bad, moving on.

It's almost like he's…sowing seed. And he knows that— just like the parable—quite a bit of the seed is going to get lost. On the other hand, every once in a while some of that seed is going to catch because it has fallen on good ground.

The approach seems a bit calloused until you look at it from the perspective of the three actors in the story. From the sower's perspective, the process is perfectly fair. The seed is spread evenly across all types of soil; every type of soil gets the same opportunity.

From the seed's perspective, it meets every challenge the same. It makes every effort to grow.

The responsibility of the outcome—of the harvest—lies squarely with the soil. It is the soil's perspective that makes all the difference. If the soil is hard and has no interest in the seed, the seed will be stolen. If the soil is shallow and has no depth, the seed may spout for a time but without good roots it will die when troubles come. And, if the soil is infested with distractions (i.e. thorns) the seed will have to compete for resources and will likely die of malnutrition.

Obviously, Jesus knew that it really doesn't matter if the truth is hidden in a parable. If it finds good ground, it will grow. If it doesn't, it won't.

Remember this the next time you feel like rolling your eyes at some of the Christians you see in the mass media. Yes, some will make you wince. Yes, some could benefit from better fashion sense. Yes, some will make you want to say, "Stop talking!"

But ultimately, those who have ears will hear because the truth is full of life and will spout soon after it hits good soil. And if the truth lands on bad soil? In that case, the truth won't grow, no matter how refined or pretty or adroit the package.

So, instead of criticizing the broadcasters, rejoice that the truth is being sown in a wide arc and carry on with your own efforts.

Of course, there are a few other observations that I'll make regarding the parable of the sower.

For one thing, when I think about the kinds of soil that Jesus describes, I find each connects easily to the activity of the flesh: the isolation of harden ground, the distractedness of the shallow soil and the noise of the cares of this world.

This is the primary reason I have given up debating theology and philosophy with others. Either the soil is ready or it's not. No amount of arguing will change that.

I also find it fascinating that Jesus didn't pre-screen those that he chose for his disciples.

He could have spent the first two years of his ministry travelling from town to town, talking to the crowds, watching for the right reactions. Once he saw the truth taking hold in certain individuals, he could have christened them part of his inner circle.

Instead, Jesus chooses twelve guys, and frankly, these guys are *not good soil*. Jesus bounces a lot of seed off them before it finally takes root. But because Jesus takes time to be with them, he has the time to plow up the hard paths. He has time to dig out the rocks and root out the thorns.

In time, he *works* them into good soil. And they produce a harvest.

So, does the broadcast work?

Absolutely.

Are there are plenty of places around the world where the broadcast is the only chance for the seed to find good soil?

Absolutely.

But make no mistake about the numbers: In the parable of the sower, *at least* three-fourths of the seed dies out. On the other hand, in Jesus' work with the disciples, eleven out of twelve produce a good crop.

What will you do with your life? Will you be content to broadcast (or simply pay someone else to broadcast)? Or, will you be willing to work the soil?

hands in the AIR scream like a GIRL

Water is an easy metaphor for life. As we move down our individual rivers we sometimes enjoy the stillness and other times slosh through the rapids. The water—the existence—that carries us through all these times remains the same yet we greet certain events with joy and others with fear.

It's easy to explain this away. We say, "There's safety in the stillness and danger in the rapids. They move too fast."

That answer deceives.

For vacation one year, my wife and I spent a week at Disney World. We willingly allowed ourselves to be strapped into carriers. These carriers spun us in circles, launched us into the air, flipped us upside down, rolled us through corkscrews and dropped us into freefall.

We loved every minute of Disney's "rapids."

Why?

Because we kept our hands and feet inside the cart "at all times"…and we trusted the ride.

Too many times in life, we fret. We allow our flesh to convince us that there's reason to fear, that God can't be trusted with the big green button.

Wouldn't we better off if we just threw our hands in the air and screamed like little girls cresting the highest peak of the rollercoaster?

When I shared this with a friend he immediately observed, "Well yeah but…going into the ride you can see people coming out and you can see that they're okay."

But, don't we have the same?

Are we not surrounded by a "great host of witness" who have gone before and found him trustworthy?

He built the universe.

He loves you.

He crafted your existence.

Enjoy the ride.

God of the mundane

A few weeks ago, my wife was preparing to host a dinner party at our house and I was doing what I could to assist. At one point, she asked me to take two pans of "Hawaiian chicken" downstairs because she wanted to use the upstairs oven for rolls.

Knowing this was one of the main courses for the meal, I carried them one at a time and rehearsed a little mantra as I went:

"Don't drop the chicken."

"Don't drop the chicken."

"Don't drop the chicken."

"Don't drop the chicken."

I managed to transport them to the oven without incident. I even set the oven to the right temperature.

And, once they finished cooking, I retraced my steps, carefully, this time with hot pads.

"Don't drop the chicken."

"Don't drop the chicken."

"Don't drop the chicken."

"Don't drop the chicken."

As I was half-way up the staircase with the first pan, a thought drifted into my spirit:

"God is the God of the mundane."

And I readily agree because it was fun to take one precise step after another, repeat my mantra and feel the Eternal grin.

As I rounded the corner to the kitchen, my wife looked up and asked, "What?"

"What," I responded, not sure what she was asking.

"You looked like you were getting ready to laugh," she explained.

I smiled. "Just thinking about Jesus," I told her.

A week and a half later, I attended a seminar by an engineer from Fermi National Accelerator Laboratory. He titled his lecture "Revolutionary Discoveries in Physics and Cosmology." It was extremely interesting and, towards the end, he told us about a presentation he had seen on the machinery that operates in the human body.

And when I say, "machinery," I mean machinery in the literal sense—motors, ratchets, transport ferries, transcription devices. They are constructed from single proteins and protein complexes. They convert chemical energy into mechanical work.

These things are tiny. They are measured in nanometers. A nanometer is one *billionth* of a meter. Humans measure one to two billion nanometers. Red blood cells measure approximately ten thousand nanometers. *E Coli* bacteria measure approximately one thousand nanometers. Viruses measure approximately one hundred nanometers. The machines that the presenter discussed measure between one and twenty nanometers.

So what do these machines do?

They make life possible.

For instance, there is a kinesin motor that literally walks chemical packages called vesicles to their destinations. Among a host of other duties, kinesin motors walk neuro-transmitter chemicals from your spinal column to your hands and feet. Studies have shown that kinesin motors operate at 70% efficiency.

And then there's ATP synthase, a molecular turbine that is powered by the passage of hydrogen protons through the membrane of a cell. It literally spins and brings together two molecules that bind to make ATP which is the fuel that runs your cells.

There's also RNA polymerase. In order for your cells to function, they must manufacture proteins to exact specifications. Those specifications are coded into each cell's copy of your DNA. When one of these proteins is needed, RNA polymerase travels along the DNA to find the right spot. It then unzips the DNA and begins crawling forward, transcribing the appropriate section, one molecule at a time, to create a string of RNA.

And if it makes a mistake? It backs up, waits for a specific chemical to come along and clip off the problem and then it resumes its transcription. This gives it an error rate of only one in one hundred thousand to one in one million.

And there are thousands and thousands and thousands of these nano-machines in every single cell of your body and they are working every moment of every day to keep you alive. The most often repeated count that I found on the Internet says that there are approximately 50 *trillion* cells in your body. That's more than the estimated number of galaxies in the universe.

The day after I went to the seminar, I drove to work in silence and thought about all the processes that were going on inside me. Obviously, I had no idea how they worked. I had no idea how many were happening simultaneously within me.

But I did know that I was a source of unbounded wonder. I could spend the entire day sitting in a chair and staring at a wall and for anyone who truly understood what was happening in my body, I would be the most fascinating thing in the room.

It gave new meaning to the phrase, "God is the God of the mundane."

Because — if the Eternal is as he is described in the Bible — the Eternal comprehends the whole of your existence, simultaneously. He sees every single process within you.

Too many times we let the flesh convince us that God will only approve of us if we follow some code or accomplish some great task.

The fact is that even when you aren't doing anything, God looks at you and says, "Wow! That's cool!" He designed you. He thinks you're spectacular, all the way from the nano-machines that keep you alive to your loftiest thoughts and greatest skills.

But at the risk of ending this chapter on an observation that will make you cringe, I must offer that God's fascination for humanity is all-inclusive. He is God of the mundane, in the literal sense.

The word "mundane" literally means "of, relating to, or characteristic of the world."

In 2 Corinthians 5:19, Paul describes the message that God has given him. It is a message of reconciliation: that God through Jesus Christ has reconciled the world to himself. He does not hold our shortcomings against us.

Just as there is nothing that you can do to make yourself more appealing to God because you're already far more fascinating than you could ever realize, neither can you do anything to make yourself any less incredible. And that observation applies to everyone, even those who have hurt you...at the very moment they were hurting you.

God is not mad at them.

God is not mad at you.

He's the God of the mundane.

TRUTH that scatters

A few days ago, I spoke with some friends in the midst of distressing times. They had received unwelcome news regarding a situation very close to their hearts.

The husband told me that while he knew intellectually that God loved him, he admitted that his emotions had been buffeted by the events and he recognized that he was developing in his experience of experiencing God.

I agreed that all of life is a process and all of us are growing but I also wanted to share with them an approach that has helped me as I have encountered the challenges of life.

So I told them this story:

As I've mentioned before, I do computer consulting for a living. I have been honored to work on important systems for a few companies around town.

No matter how much testing I do, no matter how many quality assurance checks I perform, there's always a point when the system has to be deployed. And when you're deploying a "backbone" system for a company that simply must work right, the flesh makes every attempt to fill deployment day with stress.

And so, as I drive to work that day, I use a tactic to clear the atmosphere of my mind, I take the worst consequences that my flesh can imagine and I shine truth on them—the only truth that matters.

"Father," I begin, speaking out loud in a deliberate tone, "I thank you for this day. I thank you for the help that you have provided on all the days that have led up to this day. Whatever happens today—whether all goes well or everything falls apart—I know that you are already at the end of this day and you will love me at the end of this day exactly the same as you love me right now. Whether I am disgraced today, whether I am ashamed today or whether I triumph today, all that matters to me is your love and your presence. I am yours. If there is a disaster, I will still be yours. If there is success, I will still be yours. I love you and I thank you for loving me."

Speaking the truth, hearing yourself rehearse the truth, will drive out the lies that the flesh is trying to peddle.

And it works for more than just the "big" days.

A few hours after I told my friends that story, I dropped by Wal-mart to pick up a few things. As I drove into the parking lot I remembered a conversation that I had had with another friend. As we talked about faith, he mentioned that his wife always believes for a parking spot near the door.

And as I neared the front of the store, I spotted a car pulling out from a spot right at the entrance. I smiled and slowed to a stop before turning on my blinker. Just as the car pulled out of the spot, another car came from the opposite direction and took it.

I smiled again. I don't mind walking. In fact, I enjoy walking so I quickly found another spot and wandered into the store.

Of course, my flesh started doing its little dance.

"She could see that you were waiting for that spot and she just cut in front of you! Who does she think she is…."

I ignored it and did my shopping.

But even while I was driving home, my flesh kept baiting me, kept trying to get my attention and trick me into stewing over the woman's behavior.

"Okay, that's it," I finally said before switching modes, "I thank you my God for this good day. I thank you that you provided a parking space for this woman. I noticed when she was walking into the store that she seemed to have a bit of a limp. I'm sure it was a blessing for her to find a parking place so near the store. I just ask that you bless her today and give her a great rest of the day."

As soon as I did this, the snarl within me subsided. I drove the rest of the way home in peace.

Here's why this works: Belief is the only tool that your flesh has to influence you. If your flesh can sour your soul with a falsehood, it can generate all manner of thoughts, emotions, words and actions.

If you don't recognize that this is happening, you end up wrestling with the effects of the attack and not the cause. This is what the flesh wants because no matter how disciplined you are, if you don't deal with the cause, the attack will continue.

But when you speak truth to yourself, that truth blows holes in the falsehood and once you can see through the falsehood, it loses its power to influence you.

It's like shining a light on the cockroaches. Once they know that you can see them and what they're doing, they scatter.

raised by WOLVES

(Note: I almost decided not to include this chapter even though this is something that I discuss with friends over a meal. Please remember that the point of these discussions is not accusation or condemnation. The point is to offer you possibilities that you might not have considered. It is up to you to decide if you find anything of benefit here. Please remember as well that the point of these discussions is personal. The worst use of this information would be for you to remember these words only so that you can point a finger at others.)

When my daughter was very young, I heard a visiting preacher say that the best thing I could do in my role as a father was to live fully in my own personal relationship with God. That statement calmed me because I deeply desired for my daughter to know God, to love him, to set her face towards him and never turn away. And frankly, I was looking for a way to "insure" that outcome.

Of course, each person is an individual. Each person makes his or her own choices. But I wanted to do whatever I could to create an environment where my child's spiritual life could thrive.

So, while I knew that I could never insure any of her choices, the preacher's advice seemed sound—especially since I had experienced it first-hand.

As a computer consultant, I meet my share of people. Several years ago, I was out to dinner with a client and we were chatting. I had spent enough time with him that we had moved beyond surface-level patter.

"Can I ask you a question?" he said, suddenly growing serious.

"Sure," I responded.

"Why didn't you ever turn your back on Christianity?"

I smiled and let the question hang in the air for a moment. Then I told him this story:

My parents were missionaries. For most of their careers they worked in Bible colleges in Asia. One day, my mom suggested to my dad that the school's library needed to be renovated. My dad promptly replied that he didn't have the time to take on another project and the college certainly didn't have the finances.

My mom—never one to be easily deferred—quickly announced that my dad didn't have to take on the project. Instead, she would tackle it. And, as for the finances? She said she would pray and God would supply.

Not long afterwards, my mom walked into the house waving a check for $1000.00. A pastor had written to say that he felt impressed to send the extra money. He thought my mom and dad might need it for a special project.

As I recall, my mom prayed in $15,000.00—which was a fair bit of money in the 1970s. And, during the renovations, she would gather the workers each day and they would lay their hands on the plans and mom would pray for God to give them wisdom.

It wasn't long before the project was complete and the students were enjoying the new library.

This wasn't unusual in our household. God was an ever-present partner, an ever-present resource and an ever-present friend. Every day I saw the Christian belief system provide an environment of success.

"So, why would I ever turn my back on that?" I asked my business associate, with a smile.

He shrugged and agreed that I had good reason to remain in Christ.

And remain I did. I never experienced a rebellious stage in my teenage years. I did, however, have a startling revelation or two. In the Philippines, I attended a school for missionary kids called Faith Academy. The school had a madrigal group that toured to raise money and awareness for the school. I can still remember the group's first weekend retreat. We sat in a circle, sharing prayer requests and some of the students asked the rest of us to pray that they would have a better relationship with their parents. Until that point, I just assumed that if you had Christian parents you can a good relationship with them.

You see, most days, when I came home from school my mom would say, "Come over here, Philip, and tell me about your day." In order for me to attend Faith Academy my dad had to drive me to the nearest school bus stop—which was several miles away. He would drive me there in the morning. He would come get me in the afternoon. And we'd talk.

While they certainly had areas of their Christian experience that they were working out with the proverbial "fear and trembling," I knew they loved God with their whole hearts and I knew they loved me.

Was my family perfect? No...but from what I observed my mom and dad operated more in the spirit than they did in the flesh and that made the difference in my life. Just as I hoped as a young father that it would make a difference in my daughter's life. Just as the preacher seemed to indicate that it would.

Out of my upbringing—and out of my daughter's upbringing—here's the core piece of knowledge that I can offer you with regards to raising your family.

Your family, like every other family, is composed of many voices. There is the voice of the spirit within you. There is the voice of the spirit within your spouse. There is the voice of the spirit within your son and/or your daughter. And those voices of the spirit are pure in their love for each other and their love for you. The goal of the spirit is the construction of the family unit in which each of you as individuals and all of you as a unit can thrive.

But there is also the voice of the flesh within you. There is the voice of the flesh within your spouse. And there is the voice of the flesh within your son and/or your daughter. And those voices are pure in their hatred of each other and their hatred of you. The goal of the flesh is the destruction of the family unit and each of you as individuals.

What is needed then is for you to first cultivate a greater awareness of the spirit in your life and to make a habit of responding to the spirit instead of reacting with the flesh. As you do this, your children will see an environment of success form around you.

In addition, you should apply yourself to creating an environment of success for your spouse. One of the ways that you can do this is by communicating, spending time together, and strengthening your relationship. (Remember that the flesh always seeks to isolate and the spirit always seeks to build community.)

But beyond pursuing your own relationship with the Divine, beyond pursuing your relationship with your spouse, you should seek to create an environment of success for your child. Your child's relationship with you will color their relationship with authority for the rest of their lives.

Do the things that would be obvious if you lived fully by your spirit.

For instance:

Be trustworthy. Do what you say you are going to do.

I could run through dozens of other examples but this chapter is already too long so I will summarize.

If you live by the spirit, your child will be raised by the spirit. Otherwise, your child will be raised by the wolf of your flesh.

(Recently, as I discussed this with a young father, he found the analogy of the "wolf of the flesh" interestingly appropriate. He observed that wolves travel together. Sometimes they work together. Sometimes they war. And sometimes they flip back and forth between these two states. Hopefully, this activity doesn't characterize your family.)

And if you haven't thrown this book at the wall yet, let me provide an example of the possibilities that you have in any given situation.

One morning, while eating with some friends, I offered this topic of child-raising for discussion. One of the men asked my opinion on a situation that he was facing with his son.

In his words, his son was argumentative. He would tell his son to do something and his son would drag him into in a long winded debate that would usually end with my friend saying "Just do it because I said so!"

I smiled. The flesh loves throwing its authority around. It knows that when it does this, it immediately separates "us" into "me against you." I thought for a moment, listened for a moment, and then put my arm around my friend.

As I leaned in close to him I smiled again and said, "How about this? 'Son, I have to tell you that I am amazed at the mind that God has given. You are so quick when it comes to analyzing a situation and looking at it from all angles. I have no idea what you'll choose to be when you get older. Maybe you'll be a politician. Maybe you'll be a lawyer. All I know is God has given you a great mind. But there's more at work here than you exercising your mind every time I ask you to do something. Your mom and I are also trying to create an environment of success for you, now and in the coming years. When you go out to make your way in the world, we want you to have the skills that you'll need to get and keep a job. And I can assure you that at some point along the line you're going to have bosses who are going to tell you to do something…they won't ask…they will *tell* you to do things that you're not going to want to do. And if you're going to argue over everything they tell you to do—believe me—you are not going to be able to keep a job because they will *fire* you. Learning to do what you're asked to do without argument or even bristling is a valuable skill. And when you get out there, that skill will serve you well.'"

(Okay, that's not exactly what I said, but it was the idea.)

And, why did I put my arm around my friend? Because human touch is important. Why did I lean in? Because I wanted him to know that he had my full attention.

The tactic is simple and it applies to more than just child rearing: When the flesh in another person tries to rile the flesh within you, go to quiet, listen, and then speak "spirit to spirit" (instead of reacting to their flesh which will make their flesh react to you which will make your flesh react...).

There's much more to say about this but I'm trying to keep these chapters short. Think about this.

Ask God to help you find ways to increase the life of the spirit within you, within your spouse and within your children. He will guide you if you get quiet and patient enough to hear him.

destruction
LIFE vs. LIFE

First of all, congratulations! You've made it to the last chapter. I realize there is a lot of material here and it is definitely not organized in a neat little package. Hopefully, there has been *something* useful within this great pile of words. If not, I apologize for wasting your time!

(On the other hand, if you are one of those people who skips ahead just to see how the book ends? That tactic won't work here. Beyond the first few chapters, the rest are random angles from a core framework.)

There is one last thought I'd like to address before toddling back to my own adventure.

Someday, I'm going to make a tee shirt with an electric chair on the front. Not your standard electric chair. This one will have attachments: extra straps, saw blades, needles, mallets, claws.

On the back, the tee shirt will have a simple inscription:

"It's not just heaven versus hell. It's life versus the destruct-o-matic."

At the beginning of this book I offered a quote from Jesus: "Enter through the narrow gate. For wide is the gate and broad is the road that leads to destruction, and many enter through it. But small is the gate and narrow the road that leads to life, and only a few find it." (Matthew 7:13-14 NIV)

The standard interpretation for these statements is similar to the standard interpretation for Jesus' story of the wise and foolish builders (see "Sand Castles"). It says that as long as you believe in Jesus, you've entered the narrow gate and you're on the path to life.

But, as always, it's good to consider the context of Jesus' statement.

The story of the gates occurs near the end of the Sermon on the Mount. Directly after the story, Jesus tells his listeners to watch out for false prophets, to check their fruit. He also reveals that not everyone who calls him "Lord" will enter the kingdom of heaven but only those who do God's will. And he tells the parable of the wise and foolish builder, noting that the foolish builder—the one who hears the words of Jesus but doesn't put them into practice—builds his house on a foundation that will collapse with the first storm.

I see a common theme here: Be diligent with your life because it is easy to be deceived. It's easy to live in a "disconnect" between what you say and what you do. And that disconnect has consequences.

If the story of the gates is part of the statements that follow it, Jesus is suggesting that we take stock of our lives, to determine if life or destruction surrounds us.

He doesn't do this to condemn us. He does this to encourage us to return to the small gate and the narrow path — if that's what we need to do.

Jesus knew how easy it is for us to wander from the path of life. It usually starts with some minor tilt. The flesh rarely attempts a major course correction. It is content to murmur, to sigh, to grouse, to whine, to question.

If it finds traction, it will tilt harder.

At these times, it's good to remind yourself that no amount of complaint will ever lead you to contentment, no amount of worry will ever lead you to joy and no amount of anger will ever lead you to wholeness.

But, most assuredly, entertaining those things will — step by tiny step — lead you to destruction.

I've watched this long enough that I can see destruction coming a long way away. And I have had the unhappy privilege to watch it swallow some around me. Ultimately, I cannot choose the path for you but I am hoping that something here helps you with the constant decision.

Simply put, there are only two choices in life. You can be led by the spirit. You can be led by the flesh. The first is the path to life. The second is the path to destruction.

Within every thought, every word, every deed and every action lays two gates.

Choose well.

learn3r, bail a pearl:

lest wedded inside in deed

great thoughts inspire _ _ _ _ _ _

Hints:

- The answer is exact, defensible and all-inclusive.

- Originally, the title of the chapter "Truth Bubbles" was "Truth Leaks" but that didn't work at all. Then I changed it to "Truth Oozes" because that sort-of worked. Eventually I just changed it to the current name.

- Why is the chapter "Still Whispers" unique?

- Try asking Jesus to help you (and then just do whatever pops into your head). But remember, sometimes Jesus enjoys the game "Hotter/Colder."

Made in the USA
Monee, IL
05 October 2020